Some in our culture would insist t
and ask everyone to say, "Merry C.................
appeal to believers everywhere to return to the true reason for
Christmas—the incarnation of God's Son. That is exactly what
Kate Schwarzenbart helps us do in her devotional, *Come and
Worship*. This book will challenge individuals and families to
prioritize the disciplines of reading and reflecting on the
greatest story ever told. Each daily reading has grown out of
Kate's love for the Savior and the preparation for her Bible
classes and chapels at Fox Valley Christian Academy. Keep
your copy close at hand, and then by all means come...and
worship.

Dr. Harry Shields
Adjunct Professor
Moody Theological Seminary

Kate Schwarzenbart has put together an excellent Christmas-
time devotional for families that will cause hearts to worship
and will motivate them to serve the "new-born King." Her work
is outstanding. Her devotionals give accurate, helpful
explanations of the Scripture passages. She frequently
explains the gospel through compelling commentary on the
Scripture.

Dr. Danny Leavins
Senior Pastor
Calvary Bible Church, Neenah WI

Come and Worship
Family Devotions
for the Advent Season

Kate Schwarzenbart

Come and Worship

Family Devotions for the Advent Season

Cover Photography: Kate Schwarzenbart and Tammy Muller

To the families of
Fox Valley Christian Academy
and
Calvary Bible Church.

Special thanks to Sarah Pollock, Deb Rohrkaste, Jay Schwarzenbart, Dr. Harry Shields, Dr. Danny Leavins, and the 2018 8th grade class of Fox Valley Christian Academy for editing, previewing, checking references and accuracy, and encouraging me to take to the steps to publish.

Table of Contents

Each day includes a Scripture passage, a short devotional, a challenge, and a hymn or carol to help you *come and worship.*

Day 18 – *God Chooses Mary* - Luke 1:26-35

Day 19 – *God with Us* - Isaiah 7:10-14

Day 20 – *For Unto Us a Child is Born* - Isaiah 9:2-7

Day 21 – *Elizabeth and Mary* - Luke 1:39-45

Day 22 – *The Magnificat* - Luke 1:46-56

Day 23 – *The Naming of John* - Luke 1:57-66

Day 24 – *The Benedictus* - Luke 1:67-80

Day 25 – *An Angel Appears to Joseph* - Matthew 1:18-25

Day 26 – *The Birth of Jesus* - Luke 2:1-7

Day 27 – *Hurry Shepherds, Run!* - Luke 2:8-20

Day 28 – *Simeon Blesses the Baby* - Luke 2:21-35

Day 29 – *The Visit of the Magi* - Matthew 2:1-12

Day 30 – *Out of Egypt* - Matthew 2:13-23

Day 1 – Let Every Heart Prepare Him Room

Isaiah 40:1-5

¹"Comfort, comfort my people,"
*   says your God.*
² "Speak tenderly to Jerusalem,
*   and proclaim to her*
that her hard service has been completed,
*   that her sin has been paid for,*
that she has received from the Lord's hand
*   double for all her sins."*
³ A voice of one calling:
"In the wilderness prepare
*   the way for the Lord;*
make straight in the desert
*   a highway for our God.*
⁴ Every valley shall be raised up,
*   every mountain and hill made low;*
the rough ground shall become level,
*   the rugged places a plain.*
⁵ And the glory of the Lord will be revealed,
*   and all people will see it together."*
For the mouth of the Lord has spoken.

A double portion of comfort is in store for the people of God. Though her sins are like scarlet, God's plan is to wash them white as snow (Isaiah 1:18). This prophecy, given seven hundred plus years before the birth of Christ, and over one hundred years prior to the Babylonian exile, promises a restoration for the nation of Judah. Her sins have made her a stench in the nostrils of a holy God. So much so, that *double punishment* is also in store. However, this punishment will not destroy the nation or her people. After a time of discipline, wherein God's people would lose their freedom and their national standing at the hands of Nebuchadnezzar's Babylonian Empire, God promised to bring His people out of exile and punishment and to restore their nation. The deliverance from Babylonian exile promised in Isaiah previews the salvation Jesus brings as He frees the people from slavery to sin.

Isaiah's prophecy refers to the ministry of John the Baptist who prepared the way for the coming of the Messiah (Mark 1:1-3). In the Ancient Near East, representatives went ahead of coming dignitaries to clear obstacles out of the road and announce the coming of the king. Travel was difficult in ancient times. People couldn't just get in their cars and make their way "over the river and through the woods to grandmother's house." The few roads available were dusty and dirty. They could be filled with all manner of debris from waste, to rocks, to dead animals. In addition, bandits and thieves often attacked travelers. It was important that the path be made ready for the safety of the coming king. Likewise, a visiting king would require a warm reception by the citizens. Even today, we greet traveling dignitaries, like the president, the prime minister, or the king or queen with celebrations honoring their positions. Similarly, John paved the way for Jesus, calling people to prepare themselves by repenting of their sins and turning their lives back to the Lord.

This Christmas, take time to prepare your heart by removing the obstacles that prevent you from living for the Lord, becoming more like Jesus, honoring Him as King, and building His kingdom. The false gods of security, significance, satisfaction, success, self, and stuff clutter the access points of our lives so that the sacred has little room for entry or occupancy. God will not force His way into a heart that is not prepared to receive Him. "Let every heart prepare Him room," says the popular Christmas carol, *Joy to the World*. As our hearts open and we remove the obstacles to God's reign, the glory of Lord will be revealed through us as we remember our Savior and point others to Him.

> *Joy to the world, the Lord is come*
> *Let earth receive her King*
> *Let every heart prepare Him room*
> *And heaven and nature sing*
> *And heaven and nature sing*
> *And heaven, and heaven and nature sing*

Joy to the World

Day 2 – Waiting for the Return of the King

Isaiah 52:7-10

⁷ How beautiful on the mountains
*   are the feet of those who bring good news,*
who proclaim peace,
*   who bring good tidings,*
*   who proclaim salvation,*
who say to Zion,
*   "Your God reigns!"*
⁸ Listen! Your watchmen lift up their voices;
*   together they shout for joy.*
When the Lord returns to Zion,
*   they will see it with their own eyes.*
⁹ Burst into songs of joy together,
*   you ruins of Jerusalem,*
for the Lord has comforted his people,
*   he has redeemed Jerusalem.*
¹⁰ The Lord will lay bare his holy arm
*   in the sight of all the nations,*
and all the ends of the earth will see
*   the salvation of our God.*

In a day where the written word was rare, and most people could not read, messengers were dispatched to spread good news by shouting it. When the exiles were released from Babylon (the scene described in this passage), the watchmen would have been the first to see them. Watchmen sat on the walls of the city and surveyed the surrounding country for potential enemies, returning armies, and coming visitors. It was their job to prepare the city for anything headed its way. Imagine sitting in the living room window waiting for someone special to return or to visit. Perhaps a parent or spouse has been traveling for work or grandma and grandpa are on their way. Anticipation builds during the wait and explodes in shouts of joy at the arrival of the returnee or the long-awaited guests.

The watchmen in today's passage must have felt the same way. They waited years to see the deliverance from Babylon. When they finally saw the exiles returning, the watchmen began the shouts of joy and songs of exultation that announced freedom for the captives and a time of rebuilding and restoration for the city of Jerusalem and the nation of Israel. The messengers proclaimed the sovereignty (all-powerful and right rule) of the Lord.

This passage not only declares God's sovereignty in the deliverance of His people from Babylon, but it looks forward to the peace and salvation that will find its ultimate fulfillment, not in the first coming of the Messiah that we celebrate at Christmas, but in the second coming—when Jesus, who has already achieved salvation, returns as the sovereign King over all peoples and all nations.

> *"The kingdom of this world has become the kingdom of our Lord and of his Messiah, and He will reign forever and ever."*
> *Revelation 11:15*

Today's passage describes how the watchmen became the messengers. They were prepared for action, and when the opportunity came, they led the charge! Are you watching and waiting for the salvation and return of the King? Are you aware of (and taking) the opportunities God is giving you to build His kingdom here on earth? How can you and your family proclaim the good news of the gospel in your homes, your churches, your neighborhoods, and around the world this Christmas season?

O for a thousand tongues to sing
My great Redeemer's praise
The glories of my God and King
The triumphs of His grace

My gracious Master and my God
Assist me to proclaim
To spread thru all the earth abroad
The honors of Thy name

He breaks the pow'r of canceled sin
He sets the pris'ner free
His blood can make the foulest clean
His blood availed for me

O for a Thousand Tongues to Sing

Day 3 – A Shepherd King
Isaiah 40:9-11

[9] *You who bring good news to Zion,*
go up on a high mountain.
You who bring good news to Jerusalem,
lift up your voice with a shout,
lift it up, do not be afraid;
say to the towns of Judah,
"Here is your God!"
[10] *See, the Sovereign Lord comes with power,*
and he rules with a mighty arm.
See, his reward is with him,
and his recompense accompanies him.
[11] *He tends his flock like a shepherd:*
He gathers the lambs in his arms
and carries them close to his heart;
he gently leads those that have young.

Again, Isaiah's prophecy has double fulfillment in the good news of the return from exile and the salvation brought by Christ. (It actually has triple fulfillment in the second coming.) In this passage, the prophet himself functions as the watchman and the messenger, proclaiming God leading His people out of captivity and into a new life—a message worth declaring from the mountaintops!

Isaiah makes a striking contrast in his description of the Lord. The Sovereign Lord comes in power; with a mighty arm He rules the nations as King. He brings reward, but He also pays back the evil done to His people. This God is a picture of strength. He is awesome and fearsome. He is a savior. Isaiah's word picture promised deliverance for the exiles but also foreshadowed the second coming of Christ. Revelation 19:11-16 describes the scene when the rider on the white horse, called Faithful and True, comes in power and the words from His mouth strike down His enemies as though He slew them with a sword. This rider is identified by the name inscribed on his robe and thigh:

KING OF KINGS AND LORD OF LORDS

It is this King whom Isaiah foresaw as he wrote. However, this King was not only all-powerful, He was also all-loving. Isaiah compares Him to a shepherd who gathers the lambs in His arms and carries them.

Being a shepherd was a tough job; it wasn't for the faint of heart or those who cared little for the sheep. Shepherds often slept right with their flock to guard them against dangers, and almost everything in the wild proved dangerous for sheep. There were lions and wolves and bears, not to mention robbers. There were snakes and scorpions; even the bugs relentlessly pestered the sheep. The good shepherd cared for and protected his sheep; and in turn, the sheep knew the shepherd, trusted him, and followed him. Jesus called Himself the Good Shepherd, the One who gently leads and protects His people (John 10:14).

The Jews at the time of Jesus' birth weren't waiting for a shepherd who would lead them back to God. They were waiting for a deliverer, a savior, a mighty king who would free them from the hand of Rome as God had delivered His people from Egypt and from Babylon.

Frankly, meek, mild, poor, shepherd-like Jesus was a huge disappointment for them. Many of His own people didn't recognize Him as the fulfillment of God's promise. Little did they know, everything they were hoping for in the first advent (His birth) would be completed in the second advent (His return).

Isaiah saw God as both a Savior and Shepherd. What is your picture of God? This Christmas season, how could you proclaim the good news as Isaiah did? You may not have a real mountaintop from which to shout, but God has given you a platform to share the truth. Perhaps your "mountaintop" is your workplace, your basketball team or dance troupe, the coffeeshop you frequent, or your neighbor's house. To whom will you reveal the Savior?

What child is this who laid to rest
On Mary's lap is sleeping
Whom angels greet with anthems sweet
While shepherds watch are keeping

This, this is Christ the King
Whom shepherds guard and angels sing
Haste, haste to bring Him laud
The babe, the son of Mary

So, bring Him incense, gold, and myrrh
Come peasant, king to own Him
The King of kings salvation brings
Let loving hearts enthrone Him

Raise, raise the song on high
The virgin sings her lullaby
Joy, joy for Christ is born
The babe, the son of Mary

What Child is This?

Day 4 – The Curse is Lifted
Genesis 3:8-15

[8] *Then the man and his wife heard the sound of the Lord God as he was walking in the garden in the cool of the day, and they hid from the Lord God among the trees of the garden.* [9] *But the Lord God called to the man, "Where are you?"*

[10] *He answered, "I heard you in the garden, and I was afraid because I was naked; so I hid."*

[11] *And he said, "Who told you that you were naked? Have you eaten from the tree that I commanded you not to eat from?"* [12] *The man said, "The woman you put here with me—she gave me some fruit from the tree, and I ate it."*

[13] *Then the Lord God said to the woman, "What is this you have done?"*

The woman said, "The serpent deceived me, and I ate." [14] *So the Lord God said to the serpent, "Because you have done this,*

*"Cursed are you above all livestock
    and all wild animals!
You will crawl on your belly
    and you will eat dust
    all the days of your life.*
[15] *And I will put enmity
    between you and the woman,
    and between your offspring and hers;
he will crush your head,
    and you will strike his heel."*

Every Christmas we sing *Joy to the World.* Truthfully, we often skip over the most important verse: "No more let sin and sorrows grow, nor thorns infest the ground. He comes to make His blessings known far as the curse is found!"

God's divine promise would come to earth through the womb of a woman; this chosen vessel would bear a child who would ultimately defeat Satan and sin and lift the curse God leveled on humankind.

The serpent came to Eve as a deceiver. Satan wanted Eve to believe that God was holding out on her—that His plan was unsatisfying. Eve knew better than to eat from the tree in the center of the garden, but she believed the serpent's lie that she could be just like God, knowing good and evil. And though she knew God had commanded her and her husband to not eat from the tree, she picked a fruit, took a bite, and offered some to her husband who also ate. At that moment their eyes were opened, and they realized they were naked, both physically and spiritually. Their hearts, formerly clothed with the righteousness of God, had been stripped bare. They were ashamed to stand in the presence of God; so ashamed they covered themselves with great big leaves, the only thing they could find capable of hiding their nakedness (Genesis 3:1-7).

A holy God cannot let sin go unpunished. As God walked with them in the garden that evening, He cursed the serpent, the woman, the man, and even the earth He had created. The curse of death, separation from God forever, was the result of one little lie and one little act of disobedience. And this curse didn't just affect Adam and Eve; the aftermath spread to everyone who has ever lived (Romans 5:12).

But God… Right from the very beginning of sin and separation, God had a plan to bring humanity back into righteous relationship with Himself. He would use a man, the offspring of a woman, to crush the head of the deceiver. God would plant His own seed in the womb of a young woman who would give birth to the One who would save the people from their sins.

This man, Jesus, like Adam, also represented all people. But where Adam's sin brought death, Jesus' obedience brought life and restored the right relationship between God and humankind (Romans 5:15-19).

This Jesus is the Savior, He is the King, and He is the lifter of the curse of sin. No more must the creation groan in expectation waiting for God to reveal Himself and remove the curse of sin (Romans 8:19-20). Those who have received Jesus Christ as their Savior are no longer under the curse of sin and death. Jesus' death (the death of the innocent in place of the guilty) satisfied God's anger against humanity for those who, by faith, are willing to accept His sacrifice on their behalf.

And the good news continues! Jesus didn't stay dead. The Bible teaches that after three days in the grave, He rose from the dead, defeating spiritual death (Matthew 28:6). Because of Jesus' resurrection, the sacrifice doesn't expire!

God's people were accustomed to the concept of substitutionary sacrifice. Each year, God's people sacrificed two goats on a special holiday called *Yom Kippur*, the Day of Atonement. One goat became the sacrifice and spilled its blood for the sins of the people; this goat represented a *covering over* of sin. After the blood of the first goat was used to cleanse the temple, the High Priest laid his hands on the head of the other goat (the scapegoat—the one on whom the blame was placed) and confessed over it all the sins of the people. This goat was then sent into the desert and released in a place where it would die, taking the sins of the nation with it. This represented the *removal* of sins. This ceremony satisfied God's anger against the people's unrighteousness and provided them with salvation (Leviticus 16:15-22). It was a good plan, but it was incomplete because, like a coupon, it had an expiration date. The Day of Atonement sacrifice was good for one year.

But God had a lasting solution. He sent Jesus to become the *sacrifice* and the *scapegoat* to bring us an atonement and a salvation that is complete and perfect forever. This is why we can sing, "Joy to the world, the Lord is come!"

This Christmas, have you confessed your sins to Jesus and received the *covering over* and *removal* of those sins which His sacrifice brings? The salvation of Jesus is the greatest gift anyone can receive. Have you received it?

> *No more let sin and sorrows grow*
> *Nor thorns infest the ground*
> *He comes to make His blessings known*
> *Far as the curse is found*
> *Far as the curse is found*
> *Far as, far as the curse is found*

Joy to the World

Day 5 – God Fulfills an Ancient Promise

Genesis 15:1-6

¹ After this, the word of the Lord came to Abram in a vision:
"Do not be afraid, Abram.
I am your shield,
your very great reward."

² But Abram said, "Sovereign Lord, what can you give me since I remain childless and the one who will inherit my estate is Eliezer of Damascus?" ³ And Abram said, "You have given me no children; so a servant in my household will be my heir."

⁴ Then the word of the Lord came to him: "This man will not be your heir, but a son who is your own flesh and blood will be your heir." ⁵ He took him outside and said, "Look up at the sky and count the stars—if indeed you can count them." Then he said to him, "So shall your offspring be."

⁶ Abram believed the Lord, and he credited it to him as righteousness.

In Genesis 3, God promised the serpent that the offspring of the woman would someday destroy him. God had a plan for that woman's family and it all started with a man named Abram. Abram and his wife Sarai were an elderly couple without children. They were wealthy, but they lacked the one thing they really wanted—a son, someone to carry on the family name (Genesis 11:29-30).

Years before this vision, the Lord met with Abram and asked him to leave the land of his ancestors. God also made several promises to him which can be summed up as: land, new family, and blessing (Genesis 12:1-3; 17:5-8). Abram obeyed the Lord and left the land of his father having no idea how God would take a childless couple and make them into a great nation.

Sometime later, the Lord spoke to Abram in this vision. Abram was confused by the Lord's promise because years had passed, and he and Sarai were still without a child. Abram was convinced all he owned would go to his beloved servant Eliezer, but God had a different plan. The Lord assured Abram the promised child would be conceived of his own flesh and blood and would be a true heir. Abram believed the Lord, but God kept him waiting even longer. Instead of giving him the son he desired, God gave Abram a new name, Abraham— father of many nations (Genesis 17:5-6).

When Abraham was one hundred years old, God finally gave him the son for which he was waiting. The child was called Isaac, meaning "he laughs," for his mother laughed with joy when God finally delivered on His promise (Genesis 21:1-7). Isaac married a woman named Rebecca and they had twin boys Esau and Jacob (Genesis 24-25). Jacob, though the younger of the pair, received his father's covenant blessing (the promises God made to Abraham—land, new family, and blessing) and had twelve sons of his own who became the twelve tribes of the nation of Israel (Genesis 27-30). Jacob's fourth son, Judah, is the tribe through whom Jesus, God's Son, derives His earthly lineage.

9 "You are a lion's cub, Judah;
  you return from the prey, my son.
Like a lion he crouches and lies down,
  like a lioness—who dares to rouse him?
10 The scepter will not depart from Judah,
  nor the ruler's staff from between his feet
until he to whom it belongs shall come
  and the obedience of the nations shall be his."

Genesis 49:9-10

Perhaps you've heard Jesus called "the Lion of the Tribe of Judah." That name of Jesus comes from Jacob's blessing on his son, Judah (Genesis 49:9-10). If you read the genealogies (family trees) of Christ found in Matthew 1 and Luke 3, you will see that Judah was Jesus' great-, great-, great-, great-… (you get the picture) grandfather.

When Jesus came the first time, it didn't look as though He would fulfill this prophecy. He was born in scorn, shrouded in poverty, and spent much of His life never outgrowing those labels. However, having the complete Word of God, we know that when Jesus comes a second time, He will come as the Lion of the Tribe of Judah, a ruler whose reign will never end.

God's plan of salvation and Kingship, delivered to us in a manger some 2000 years ago, has been in the works since the creation of the world. God even picked the family through whom He would build His kingdom.

Seeing the family tree of Jesus reminds us of how God works in the details, and even the waiting, of our lives. It reminds us that God is faithful to His promises, even when we aren't all that faithful (Genesis 16:1-15; 38:1-30). How have you seen God's faithfulness in your life? Remind yourself and others of the ways God has answered your prayers, how He has protected you, and how, like a shepherd, He has led you. Rehearse His faithfulness as often as possible.

My hope is built on nothing less
Than Jesus' blood and righteousness
I dare not trust the sweetest frame
But wholly lean on Jesus' name

> *On Christ the solid Rock I stand*
> *All other ground is sinking sand*
> *All other ground is sinking sand*

When darkness seems to hide His face
I rest on His unchanging grace
In ev'ry high and stormy gale
My anchor holds within the veil

> *On Christ the solid Rock I stand*
> *All other ground is sinking sand*
> *All other ground is sinking sand*

The Solid Rock

Day 6 – Prophet, Priest, and King
Deuteronomy 18:15-18

[15] "The Lord your God will raise up for you a prophet like me from among your fellow Israelites. You must listen to him. [16] For this is what you yourselves requested of the Lord your God when you were assembled at Mount Sinai. You said, 'Don't let us hear the voice of the Lord our God anymore or see this blazing fire, for we will die.'"

[17] "Then the Lord said to me," 'What they have said is right. [18] I will raise up a prophet like you from among their fellow Israelites. I will put my words in his mouth, and he will tell the people everything I command him.'"

Moses was a prophet whom biblical scholars call a "type" or a model of Jesus. God used the ministry of Moses to bring salvation for His people, Israel, who were slaves to the Egyptians. Through a series of plagues and miracles, God delivered His people from the oppressive and evil control of the pharaohs. Moses was considered a "friend of God" and spoke with Him as a man speaks to another man (Exodus 33:11). Moses was able to have a glimpse of the glory of God, and his face shone for months after having been in the presence of the Lord. The people were terrified, and Moses was forced to veil his face (Exodus 33:12-23; 34:29-35).

Seeing Moses' face reflecting the glory of God helped the people recognize their helpless, unrighteous state. They saw their unfitness to stand before a holy God and realized they needed someone to intercede. God responded to their need by establishing the priesthood and calling more prophets who would speak to the people on His behalf. Moses himself also made several intercessions before God to forestall the Lord's judgment on the people's sins (Exodus 32:31-32; Numbers 11:1-3; 12:9-15; 14:10-16; 21:4-9).

This passage has fulfillment in the many prophets who followed Moses, Samuel, Elijah, Elisha, Isaiah, Jeremiah, and a host of others who brought the people words from the Lord. Prior to the resurrection of Christ, the high priest also went before God and made sacrifices and intercession for the people because they could not go to God without someone acting on their behalf. Once a year, on the Day of Atonement, he entered the Most Holy Place (which was so special it was separated from the Holy Place and the rest of the temple by a thick curtain) and made the sacrifices to cover over and remove sins (Leviticus 16).

When Jesus came, He brought an even greater fulfillment to the office of prophet (see Hebrews 3 where Jesus is compared to Moses), but moreover, He also assumed the roles of High Priest and King (Hebrews 4:14-5:10).

When Jesus was crucified, the curtain separating common man from God was torn in two (Matthew 27:50-51). Through Jesus, we now have direct access to God through prayer and through His Word. In Jesus, God's plan for restoring His people was completed once and for all.

> *11 Under the old covenant, the priest stands and ministers before the altar day after day, offering the same sacrifices again and again, which can never take away sins. 12 But our High Priest offered himself to God as a single sacrifice for sins, good for all time. Then he sat down in the place of honor at God's right hand. 13 There he waits until his enemies are humbled and made a footstool under his feet. 14 For by that one offering he forever made perfect those who are being made holy.*

> *Hebrews 10:11-14*

The Old Testament painted pictures of how God's plan of salvation would be realized. The paintings were often just small samples of the much larger picture. In the prophets, the priests, and the kings, the people saw bits and pieces of who Jesus would be. Like the prophets, Jesus would speak for God; like the priests, He would stand before God in the place of humanity as the acceptable sacrifice; and like the kings, Jesus will someday "rule the world with truth and grace" and will "make the nations prove the glories of His righteousness and wonders of His love." Spend some time today thanking God for sending His Son to stand in your place as did the prophets and the priests of long ago.

> *He rules the world with truth and grace*
> *And makes the nations prove*
> *The glories of his righteousness*
> *And wonders of His love*
> *And wonders of His love*
> *And wonders, wonders of His love*

> *Joy to the World*

Day 7 – From the House of David

Psalm 89:1-4

1 *I will sing of the Lord's unfailing love forever!*
   Young and old will hear of your faithfulness.
2 *Your unfailing love will last forever.*
   Your faithfulness is as enduring as the heavens.
3 *The Lord said, "I have made a covenant with David, my chosen servant.*
   I have sworn this oath to him:
4 *'I will establish your descendants as kings forever;*
   they will sit on your throne from now until eternity.'"

King David was the second king of the nation of Israel. Like Jesus, he was also part of the family tree of Jacob's son, Judah (Matthew 1). David was the best king in Israel's history. He was a man after God's own heart (1 Samuel 13:14). He was not a perfect man, but he understood his sin, confessed it, and tried to honor the Lord (2 Samuel 11-12).

One of David's desires was to build a permanent house for the Lord. The Ark of the Covenant (the place where God's presence lived on earth) had dwelt in a moveable tabernacle since the days of Moses. By David's time, it wasn't even in the tabernacle but was stationed at the home of Obed Edom, a citizen who lived outside of Jerusalem. David brought the ark to Jerusalem amidst great celebration (2 Samuel 6).

When the ark reached Jerusalem, David told the prophet, Nathan, that he wanted to build a temple, a permanent house for God (2 Samuel 7). Nathan approved David's plan but was told in a dream that David would not be the one to build the temple. Nathan went back to David with even better news. He said, "God has decided that instead of you building a house for Him, He will build a house for you."

> *12 "For when you die and are buried with your ancestors, I will raise up one of your descendants, your own offspring, and I will make his kingdom strong. 13 He is the one who will build a house—a temple—for my name. And I will secure his royal throne forever. 14 I will be his father, and he will be my son. If he sins, I will correct and discipline him with the rod, like any father would do. 15 But my favor will not be taken from him as I took it from Saul, whom I removed from your sight. 16 Your house and your kingdom will continue before me for all time, and your throne will be secure forever."*
>
> *2 Samuel 7:12-16*

God promised David a descendent of his would reign forever in Israel. Jesus is the final king in the line of David, and He will reign forever and ever. David, another "type" of Jesus, delivered and saved his people from their enemies and brought peace to Israel. Jesus delivers and saves us from our enemy, Satan, and brings us peace with God through His sacrifice on the cross.

This psalm is another example of the Hebrew Scriptures being fulfilled in the life of Christ. Take a minute to thank God that every detail prophesied about the birth of His Son was literally and completely fulfilled.

> *God rest ye merry gentlemen*
> *Let nothing you dismay*
> *Remember Christ our Savior*
> *Was born on Christmas Day*
> *To save us all from Satan's power*
> *When we were gone astray*
> *O tidings of comfort and joy, comfort and joy*
> *O tidings of comfort and joy*

God Rest Ye Merry Gentlemen

Day 8 – A Rose Blooms

Isaiah 11:1-10

¹ *A shoot will come up from the stump of Jesse;*
  from his roots a Branch will bear fruit.
² *The Spirit of the Lord will rest on him—*
  the Spirit of wisdom and of understanding,
  the Spirit of counsel and of might,
  the Spirit of the knowledge and fear of the Lord—
³ *and he will delight in the fear of the Lord.*
He will not judge by what he sees with his eyes,
  or decide by what he hears with his ears;
⁴ *but with righteousness he will judge the needy,*
  with justice he will give decisions for the poor of the earth.
He will strike the earth with the rod of his mouth;
  with the breath of his lips he will slay the wicked.
⁵ *Righteousness will be his belt*
  and faithfulness the sash around his waist.
⁶ *The wolf will live with the lamb,*
  the leopard will lie down with the goat,
the calf and the lion and the yearling together;
  and a little child will lead them.
⁷ *The cow will feed with the bear,*
  their young will lie down together,
  and the lion will eat straw like the ox.
⁸ *The infant will play near the cobra's den,*
  and the young child will put its hand into the viper's nest.
⁹ *They will neither harm nor destroy*
  on all my holy mountain,
for the earth will be filled with the knowledge of the Lord
  as the waters cover the sea.
¹⁰ *In that day the Root of Jesse will stand as a banner for the peoples; the nations will rally to him, and his resting place will be glorious.*

Israel reached its low point as a nation when the southern kingdom of Judah fell in 586 B.C. The best and the brightest were carried off to Babylon to be acclimated into the Babylonian system. The temple was looted and destroyed, and the city was sacked (Daniel 1:1-5). The everlasting kingdom promised to David (the son of Jesse) looked to be in serious jeopardy and perhaps beyond repair. Isaiah foresaw the exile, but he also spoke of a coming restoration. This prophecy tells of a Messiah, an anointed one, who would someday restore Israel and bring its people home to the promised land.

While this promise of a future kingdom was exciting, it was very distant. God didn't intend to discipline His people from the moment of exile until the second coming of the Messiah. Like many others, this prophesy has double fulfillment. About fifty years after the destruction of the temple, the Persian Empire defeated Babylon. New rulers, Cyrus and Darius, instituted Persian policy over the nation of Israel. Persian foreign policy allowed defeated nations to remain in or return to their homelands. Darius authorized and financed the return to Judah and the rebuilding of Yahweh's temple. Another man in the line of David, Zerubbabel, led the charge in the rebuilding and the restoration. Many Jews wondered if he was the Messiah. While Zerubbabel was messianic in nature and did promote spiritual revival in the rebuilding of the temple, he wasn't the anointed one who would bring salvation and peace on earth (Haggai 1:12-15; 2:20-23).

While Isaiah's words found partial fulfillment in the return from exile, they will find complete fulfillment in the second coming of the Messiah when Jesus returns to the earth as the Davidic King. Jesus will be sovereign over all nations, over all peoples, and over all creation, so much so that children will be able to play with animals that are currently deadly. The Messianic kingdom will be a kingdom of peace and righteousness because Satan will be bound, and sin will be very limited in its scope and influence (Revelation 20:1-6).

Though the nation of Israel rejected Jesus as their Messiah during His first advent, God is not done with them. Many biblical scholars believe God will remove His church from the earth (though the rapture) and work specifically with the nation of Israel to restore and redeem them during a time of tribulation on the earth (1 Thessalonians 4:13-5:11).

This passage brings tremendous hope to those who are walking through times of difficulty. God allows seasons of pain and suffering to enter the lives of those He loves to drive them back to Himself (Hebrews 12:7-12). The discipline of the exile did indeed drive Israel back towards a life that was increasingly pleasing to the Lord. Whether this Christmas finds you in a season of blessing or trial, God is not finished with you. As He remakes creation, He is remaking individuals and conforming them to His image (2 Corinthians 5:17). How is God at work in your life to make you more like Jesus?

Lo! How a Rose e'er blooming
From tender spring hath sprung
Of Jesse's lineage coming
As men of old have sung
There came a flower bright
Amid the cold of winter
When half gone was the night

Lo! How a Rose E'er Blooming

Day 9 – Salvation Spring Up

Zechariah 6:12-13

12 Tell him this is what the Lord Almighty says: 'Here is the man whose name is the Branch, and he will branch out from his place and build the temple of the Lord. 13 It is he who will build the temple of the Lord, and he will be clothed with majesty and will sit and rule on his throne. And he will be a priest on his throne. And there will be harmony between the two.'

Jewish sources tell us that this passage was considered messianic in its original delivery. The prophet Zechariah was instructed to have a crown prepared for the head of Joshua, the high priest. This crown headpiece was different from the turban normally worn by the high priest and united, in symbolic form, the offices of high priest and king. The names Joshua and Jesus come from the same root and mean "the Lord saves." The writer of Hebrews calls Jesus a High Priest in the Order of Melchizedeck, who was both the king and the high priest in Salem during Abram's time (Genesis 14:18-20; Hebrews 5:5-6).

The prophecy spoken here was given to Joshua and speaks of a *Branch* that would grow out and be responsible for the rebuilding of the temple. In Isaiah's prophecy, the Messiah is referred to as a "shoot from the root of Jesse." Later, Isaiah refers to salvation springing up from the ground as does new growth during the spring.

> *"You heavens above, rain down my righteousness; let the clouds shower it down. Let the earth open wide, let salvation spring up, let righteousness flourish with it; I, the LORD, have created it."*
>
> *Isaiah 45:8*

The root of Jesse, the line of David, though it looked dead due to the exile, continued to live underground until the spring of new beginnings in God's plan of salvation.

The high priest Joshua was highly involved with Zerubbabel in the rebuilding of the temple. The words he received promised that the *Branch* would build the temple. From this side of history, we know that Christ is the *Branch* and the *temple* of God (John 2:12-22). But it goes beyond that. In Christ, those who have received Him are part of His glorious kingdom and will reign with Him as kings and priests (Revelation 5:10). Peter says this of the church:

But you are a chosen people, a royal priesthood, a holy nation, God's special possession, that you may declare the praises of him who called you out of darkness into his wonderful light.

1 Peter 2:9

Jesus was the temple of God while He walked on earth; we, as believers in Christ, have the Holy Spirit in us. The Holy Spirit, the third person of the Trinity, tabernacles (dwells) in each individual believer making us the temple of God as well (John 14:16-17; Acts 2:1-4).

Because of the *Branch*, we can be in tune with the work of the Lord and build His kingdom here on earth. What is one specific way your family can participate in God's kingdom work this Christmas season?

O holy night the stars are brightly shining
It is the night of the dear Savior's birth
Long lay the world in sin and error pining
Till He appeared and the soul felt its worth
A thrill of hope the weary world rejoices
For yonder breaks a new and glorious morn
Fall on your knees oh hear the angel voices
O night divine, O night when Christ was born
O night, O holy night, O night divine

Truly He taught us to love one another
His law is love and His gospel is peace
Chains He shall break for the slave is our brother
And in His name all oppression shall cease
Sweet hymns of joy in grateful chorus raise we
Let all within us praise His holy name
Christ is the Lord, O praise His name forever
His power and glory ever more proclaim
His power and glory ever more proclaim

O Holy Night

Day 10 – The Bethlehem Connection

Micah 5:2-4

²*"But you, Bethlehem Ephrathah,*
though you are small among the clans of Judah,
out of you will come for me
one who will be ruler over Israel,
whose origins are from of old,
from ancient times."
³*Therefore Israel will be abandoned*
until the time when she who is in labor bears a son,
and the rest of his brothers return
to join the Israelites.
⁴*He will stand and shepherd his flock*
in the strength of the Lord,
in the majesty of the name of the Lord his God.
And they will live securely, for then his greatness
will reach to the ends of the earth.

Have you ever wondered, "Why Bethlehem?" Why on earth would God choose to deliver the greatest gift of all time in a backwoods hamlet seven miles south of Jerusalem? As it turns out, Bethlehem is far more significant than many people think. It was, indeed, a small town, 500-600 people at most. Though it was small, it was not new. The patriarch Jacob's wife, Rachel, was buried in Bethlehem (Genesis 35:19-20). Nineteen hundred years before the birth of Christ, this tiny village was already connected to the covenant God made with Abraham, Israel (Jacob), and David. Furthermore, we learn in Ruth that her father-in-law Elimelech was from Bethlehem; when Ruth and Naomi returned from Moab, they settled right back in Bethlehem (Ruth 1:1-2).

Ruth's story is a very important stopping point. Ruth was the third Gentile (non-Jewish) woman grafted into the family tree of Jesus (Matthew 1:5). Ruth's rescue by Boaz is a story which parallels and previews the rescue mission of Jesus Christ (Ruth 2-4). Boaz is another "type" of Christ. Ruth is a "type" of humanity. Both Ruth's redemption and the birth of the Redeemer of all humanity happened in Bethlehem.

The story makes another important stop in Bethlehem when Ruth's great-grandson, David, was anointed king of Israel by the prophet Samuel (1 Samuel 16:1-13). God chose a shepherd to become the next king. The humble was exalted, the weak made strong, and the least likely chosen. David was also a "type" of Christ.

After the reign of King David (1010-970 BC) and Micah's prophecy from around 750 BC, we don't hear of Bethlehem again until the Roman Emperor, Caesar Augustus, ordered a census and sent everyone to his hometown to register. We learn in Luke that Jesus' father, Joseph, was part of the family line of David from Bethlehem; thus, the family made the trip there to register for the census (Luke 2:4).

Since people had several months to complete the requirements of the census, it is likely Joseph and Mary combined their trip to Bethlehem with their required pilgrimage to Passover. It was substantial journey they wouldn't have wanted to make twice, especially with Mary being pregnant.

The journey to Bethlehem most likely did not take place in the dead of winter like our Christmas holiday. We celebrate Christmas in late December because the Roman Catholic Church wanted to provide an alternative to the pagan holidays surrounding the winter solstice (December 20-21).[1] However, it is unlikely Jesus was born in December. December wasn't lambing season and shepherds would not have been watching their flocks by night. Most scholars believe Jesus was born in the spring, probably around Passover (March or April).

The final reference to Bethlehem is from John's gospel which confirms the people expected the Messiah to be from Bethlehem as the prophecy foretold (John 7:42).

The little town of Bethlehem was connected to the Messianic Covenant for nearly 2000 years! The Shepherd King is our Redeemer and the Old Testament references to Bethlehem tell the whole story hundreds of years before it happens. Our God is in the details!

Praise God for sending us His Son! Take some time to thank God for the intricate ways He tells His stories. Thank Him for including you in His plan of redemption!

---

[1] For a fun family look at the history of Christmas, check out Phil Vischer's *Buck Denver Asks, Why Do We Call it Christmas?* https://www.rightnowmedia.org/Content/Series/397#1. The DVD can also be purchased on Amazon.

O little town of Bethlehem
How still we see thee lie
Above thy deep and dreamless sleep
The silent stars go by
Yet in thy dark streets shineth
The Everlasting Light
The hopes and fears of all the years
Are met in thee tonight

For Christ was born of Mary
And gathered all above
While mortals sleep
The angels keep their watch of wondering love
O morning stars together
Proclaim Thy holy birth
And praises sing to God our King
And peace to men on earth

How silently, how silently
The wondrous gift is giv'n
So, God imparts to human hearts
The blessings of His heaven
No ear may hear His calling
But in this world of sin
Where meek souls will receive Him still
The dear Christ enters in

O Holy Child of Bethlehem
Descend on us we pray
Cast out our sin and enter in
Be born in us today
We hear the Christmas angels
Their great glad tidings tell
O come to us, abide with us
Our Lord Emmanuel

O Little Town of Bethlehem

Day 11 – Refiner's Fire

Malachi 3:1-4

[1] "I will send my messenger, who will prepare the way before me. Then suddenly the Lord you are seeking will come to his temple; the messenger of the covenant, whom you desire, will come," says the Lord Almighty.

[2] But who can endure the day of his coming? Who can stand when he appears? For he will be like a refiner's fire or a launderer's soap. [3] He will sit as a refiner and purifier of silver; he will purify the Levites and refine them like gold and silver. Then the Lord will have men who will bring offerings in righteousness, [4] and the offerings of Judah and Jerusalem will be acceptable to the Lord, as in days gone by, as in former years.

The book of Malachi, the final word of God before the birth of Jesus, centers around worship. After the exile, the people returned to Jerusalem, rebuilt the temple and the walls, and settled into a time of heavy spirituality but little real devotion. Much of Malachi is God presenting a courtroom-style case against His people. God makes an accusation and the people respond in a somewhat sarcastic manner. Then God reiterates His accusation and presents supporting evidence for His claims. The message of Malachi is simple: return to Me with all your heart.

After the exile, God's people were very concerned with the *cultus*, the religious practices surrounding their faith. However, despite their concern for carrying out the practice, they did it very half-heartedly. God accused His people of bringing diseased and blemished sacrifices (Malachi 1:6-14). He accused the priests of leading the people in sin instead of instructing them in righteousness (Malachi 2:1-9). He accused them of breaking covenant faith with Him and with their spouses (Malachi 2:10-16). He accused them of robbing Him by bringing only a portion of the prescribed offerings (Malachi 3:6-12). Though the people were completing the religious ceremonies, their hearts were far from God. A change was a necessary.

John the Baptist, the forerunner to Jesus, had a message similar to the book of Malachi. John also called people to repent of their sins, turn to God, and be baptized, publicly declaring their allegiance to Yahweh, the covenant God of Israel (Matthew 3:1-3; Luke 3:3-6). This passage in Malachi foreshadows the repentance preached by John and Jesus himself, but it refers even more specifically to the "day of the Lord," when Jesus will return to the earth as the righteous judge.

The people were waiting for a deliverer to rescue them from the hands of their enemies, but God was more concerned with their rescue from sin. He wanted them to be acceptable before Him. He wanted to clean them and purify them as a refiner purifies silver and gold. He did this by sending His Son to become sin on their behalf, taking the punishment they deserved. Paul speaks to this in his second letter to the church in Corinth.

> *God made Him who had no sin to be sin for us, so that in Him, we might become the righteousness of God.*
>
> *2 Corinthians 5:21*

Because of what God, in His Son Jesus, has done on our behalf, we have an obligation and a responsibility to allow Him to purify us. The process of purification is a long and difficult one. The refiner heats the metal to extreme temperatures to separate the pure metal from the dross (the impurities). Then he scrapes the dross off the top and heats it again. He does this over and over until he can see his face reflecting in the liquid metal. When he sees his face, he knows the metal is pure and the process is complete.

Sometimes, God puts us in the fire of affliction and suffering. During these times, He is working to purify our hearts and make us ready and fit for His Kingdom. God does not give up on us. Though we deserve His wrath, He pours out His love. His love may not always be comfortable, but He is conforming us to His own likeness and purifying us until He can see His reflection in our lives (2 Corinthians 3:18).

Is your heart refined and ready this Christmas season, or are you going through the spiritual motions while your heart is more devoted to yourself than to God? Malachi reminds us that God requires our best because He gave His best on our behalf. Let Him conform you to His image. Make your worship genuine and serve Him from a heart overflowing with thankfulness.

When peace like a river
Attendeth my way
When sorrows like sea billows roll
Whatever my lot
Thou hast taught me to say
It is well
It is well with my soul

> *It is well with my soul*
> *It is well*
> *It is well with my soul*

Tho' Satan should buffet
Tho' trials should come
Let this blest assurance control
That Christ hath regarded
My helpless estate
And hath shed His own blood
For my soul

> *It is well with my soul*
> *It is well*
> *It is well with my soul*

It is Well with My Soul

Day 12 – Light of the World

John 1:1-8

[1] *In the beginning was the Word, and the Word was with God, and the Word was God.* [2] *He was with God in the beginning.* [3] *Through him all things were made; without him nothing was made that has been made.* [4] *In him was life, and that life was the light of all mankind.* [5] *The light shines in the darkness, and the darkness has not overcome it.*

[6] *There was a man sent from God whose name was John.* [7] *He came as a witness to testify concerning that light, so that through him all might believe.* [8] *He himself was not the light; he came only as a witness to the light.*

_J_ohn's gospel is quite different from the other three gospels. Matthew, Mark, and Luke are called *synoptic gospels*. Synoptic means "to see in a like manner." Matthew, Mark, and Luke offer many parallel accounts and biographical images of Jesus' ministry, but John focuses his gospel on the person of Jesus. John lists seven signs, or proofs, that Jesus is God:

- Changing water into wine at the wedding in Cana (John 2:1-11)
- Healing the royal official's son (John 4:46-54)
- Healing the paralyzed man at the pool of Bethesda in Jerusalem (John 5:1-15)
- Feeding the 5,000 (John 6:5-14)
- Walking on water (John 6:16-25)
- Healing the man born blind (John 9:1-12)
- Raising Lazarus from the dead (John 11:1-45)

He also records seven "I Am" statements to show who Jesus is:

- Bread of Life (John 6:35)
- Light of the World (John 8:12)
- The Gate (John 10:9)
- The Good Shepherd (John 10:11, 14)
- The Resurrection and the Life (John 11:35)
- The Way, the Truth, and the Life (John 14:6)
- The Vine (John 15:5)

These are all in addition to his opening remarks that prove Jesus is the Son of God and is equal to God in every way.

Jesus, the incarnate (physical) Word of God was present with God and the Holy Spirit at creation. If you look closely, you'll notice all the pronouns in Genesis 1 and 2 are plural. The triune God (God the Father, Jesus Christ the Son, and the Holy Spirit) existed from before time began. It was through Jesus that all life took its form and breath.

Paul's letter to the church at Colosse, actually written prior to John's gospel, affirms the same message. All life is through Jesus and for Jesus. In Jesus, all things hold together.

> *15 The Son is the image of the invisible God, the firstborn over all creation. 16 For in him all things were created: things in heaven and on earth, visible and invisible, whether thrones or powers or rulers or authorities; all things have been created through him and for him. 17 He is before all things, and in him all things hold together.*
>
> *Colossians 1:15-17*

The very first thing God put into creation was light; the light came before the sun, moon, and stars which were created on day four (Genesis 1:3,14-19). John tells us Jesus claimed to be the Light of the World (John 8:12). The first thing God put into His creation was Himself. God pierced the darkness of the primeval universe with His presence and life.

But sin and death entered the world (Genesis 3:1-7) and darkness gained a foothold and continued to expand its grip until *every inclination of man was only evil all the time* (Genesis 6:5). This grieved God to the extent that His rescue mission had to be previewed. He chose Noah, a righteous man, and saved him and his family from the flood He sent as a consequence for sin (Genesis 6-7).

Since the day when Adam and Eve chose darkness over light, darkness has dominated humanity. From the tower of Babel, to a divided kingdom, to the nations of Israel and Judah falling to Assyria and Babylon, to the Greeks and the Romans, to the Crusades, and madmen like Hitler and Stalin, darkness seems to reign in the world.

But God promised,

> *The people walking in darkness have seen a great light; on those living in the land of deep darkness, a light has dawned.*

Isaiah 9:2

The darkness will never overcome the light. It may obscure it for a time, but the Light of the World will win!

As you light the tree and your homes this Christmas season, may you remember that Jesus is the Light of the World. As the small lights of Christmas bring visibility to the dark places in your home, will you allow Jesus to bring light and life to the dark places in your heart? Will you bring that light to others this Christmas?

> *Silent night, holy night*
> *All is calm, all is bright*
> *Round yon virgin mother and Child*
> *Holy Infant so tender and mild*
> *Sleep in heavenly peace*
> *Sleep in heavenly peace*
>
> *Silent night, holy night*
> *Son of God, love's pure light*
> *Radiant beams from Thy holy face*
> *With the dawn of redeeming grace*
> *Jesus Lord at Thy birth*
> *Jesus Lord at Thy birth*

Silent Night

Day 13 – Incarnation—God in the Flesh
John 1:9-18

⁹ The true light that gives light to everyone was coming into the world. ¹⁰ He was in the world, and though the world was made through him, the world did not recognize him. ¹¹ He came to that which was his own, but his own did not receive him.

*¹² Yet to all who did receive him, to those who believed in his name, he gave the right to become children of God—
¹³ children born not of natural descent, nor of human decision or a husband's will, but born of God.*

¹⁴ The Word became flesh and made his dwelling among us. We have seen his glory, the glory of the one and only Son, who came from the Father, full of grace and truth.

¹⁵ (John testified concerning him. He cried out, saying, "This is the one I spoke about when I said, 'He who comes after me has surpassed me because he was before me.'")

¹⁶ Out of his fullness we have all received grace in place of grace already given. ¹⁷ For the law was given through Moses; grace and truth came through Jesus Christ. ¹⁸ No one has ever seen God, but the one and only Son, who is himself God and is in closest relationship with the Father, has made him known.

*I*ncarnation: God clothing Himself in humanity and coming to dwell on earth. The very thought is mind-boggling. God, the Creator of a perfect world choosing to live in the mess humans made by rejecting Him. Emmanuel, God with us. The eternal God, to whom John the Baptist gave testimony, walked the earth for over thirty years, but very few saw Him for who He was. John's gospel was written to emphasize the deity, the God-likeness, of Jesus.

John goes out of his way to confirm that though the Jews knew what to expect in the Messiah, (even King Herod knew of the prophecies [Matthew 2:3-6]), they failed to realize He was among them (John 7:42). They were walking in the very presence of God, but instead of recognizing Jesus for who He was, they accused Him of having a demon (John 8:48-53). Even his family and the people of His village rejected him (Mark 6:4).

This fulfilled Isaiah's prophecy:

> *1 Who has believed our message*
> *and to whom has the arm of the Lord been revealed?*
> *2 He grew up before him like a tender shoot,*
> *and like a root out of dry ground.*
> *He had no beauty or majesty to attract us to him,*
> *nothing in his appearance that we should desire him.*
> *3 He was despised and rejected by mankind,*
> *a man of suffering, and familiar with pain.*
> *Like one from whom people hide their faces*
> *he was despised, and we held him in low esteem.*

Isaiah 53:1-3

What would we do if Jesus walked the earth today? Probably the same thing we do to anyone we consider too radical... tolerate them in person and condemn them for being self-righteous behind their backs. Jesus took the Jewish law to a whole new level.

The people were quite content with the rabbi's interpretations of the Law of Moses. They knew it couldn't be kept in its entirety, so they diluted it and created oral traditions that were possible to keep under their own power. Jesus entered the picture, condemned the Pharisees and teachers of the law, and elevated the standards for holy living to such a level that it was impossible to achieve them apart from the power of God (Matthew 23).

Blessed are the poor in the spirit—those who realize their helplessness

Blessed are those who mourn—those who feel real, grieving sorrow that leads to repentance over their sin

Blessed are the meek—those who have power, but control it

Blessed are those who hunger and thirst for righteousness—those who desire to please God more than they desire to please themselves

Blessed are the merciful—those who forgive people who don't deserve to be forgiven

Blessed are the pure in heart —those who intentionally keep themselves from things they know are less than God's best

Blessed are the peacemakers—those who love their neighbor even if they're not loved in return

Blessed are those who are persecuted—those who choose to suffer rather than compromise

From Matthew 5:3-10

Indeed, Jesus was a radical! It's no wonder many people rejected Him. God was among them, but because their hearts were hard and bent towards living for themselves, they failed to recognize the greatest gift ever given.

We must recognize Jesus and recognize our great need for Him. We are lost, condemned, and dead sinners, and God condescends to live, not just *among* us, but *in* us in the person of the Holy Spirit. The Spirit makes us alive and empowers us to live holy lives and do the work of the kingdom (Ephesians 1:18-20).

During this season of pretty lights on dark nights, see Jesus, but show Jesus as well. A single candle will go a long way to light a dark room. This Christmas season, you might be the only Jesus someone sees. Live in the power of God with us and God in us! What is one way you can live in this power and show Jesus today?

> *Yea Lord, we greet Thee*
> *Born this happy morning*
> *Jesus, to Thee be all glory giv'n*
> *Word of the Father*
> *Now in flesh appearing*
>
> > *O come let us adore Him*
> > *O come let us adore Him*
> > *O come let us adore Him*
> > *Christ Lord*

O Come All Ye Faithful

Day 14 – A Reason to Rejoice

Zechariah 9:9-13

⁹ Rejoice greatly, Daughter Zion!
*   Shout, Daughter Jerusalem!*
See, your king comes to you,
*   righteous and victorious,*
lowly and riding on a donkey,
*   on a colt, the foal of a donkey.*
¹⁰ I will take away the chariots from Ephraim
*   and the warhorses from Jerusalem,*
*   and the battle bow will be broken.*
He will proclaim peace to the nations.
*   His rule will extend from sea to sea*
*   and from the River to the ends of the earth.*
¹¹ As for you, because of the blood of my covenant with you,
*   I will free your prisoners from the waterless pit.*
¹² Return to your fortress, you prisoners of hope;
*   even now I announce that I will restore twice as much to*
you.
¹³ I will bend Judah as I bend my bow
*   and fill it with Ephraim.*
I will rouse your sons, Zion,
*   against your sons, Greece,*
*   and make you like a warrior's sword.*

Zechariah recorded his book of prophecy after the return from exile. While the nation of Israel was no longer in captivity, they weren't exactly free, and freedom was also not in the near-future. The people lived in their own land but were ruled as a puppet government of Persia. In the same way a puppeteer uses strings to manipulate a marionette, the government of Persia used its influence to control the people of Israel.

Eventually, Persia was conquered by the young Greek general, Alexander the Great, who took over much of eastern Europe, the Middle East, Western Asia, and Northern Africa. Part of the Greek policy for conquered nations was to institute Greek culture amongst the conquered people. This is called Hellenization and is the reason the New Testament is largely written in Greek rather than Hebrew or Aramaic, which were the primary languages of Israel. The Greeks also introduced worship of their pagan gods. Though Alexander died young and his empire was divided amongst his top four generals, the Hellenization continued. Israel was controlled by the Ptolemy Dynasty of Egypt until they were conquered by the Seleucid Kings who were downright cruel to God's people. Antiochus Epiphanes IV was particularly awful: it is said that he sacrificed a pig, an animal that was considered unclean to God's people, on the altar of God and set up a statue of Zeus in the temple. Many scholars believe this is an early fulfillment of Daniel's prophecy of "an abomination that causes desolation" (Daniel 11:29-32). Most scholars believe the antichrist will commit a similar offense in the new temple built during the time of tribulation (Matthew 24:15).

It was after Antiochus desecrated the temple that a man named Judah Maccabee, the son of a rural priest, Matthias, who refused to worship the Greek gods, led a revolt against the Seleucid dynasty (167-160 BC). Relying primarily on guerilla warfare techniques, the small army of Jews was able to overthrow the Greek and Syrian oppressors who were actively Hellenizing (paganizing) their culture.

Part of Judah Maccabee's goal was to cleanse the temple. He encouraged his followers to rebuild the altar and to keep the menorah burning for seven straight nights, one week's worth. God did even better. The Talmud, an important text in Judaism, speaks of the miracle in the temple. There was only enough oil to keep the menorah's candles burning for one day, but the flames continued to burn for eight nights until they were able to obtain a fresh supply of oil. This miracle led the Jewish leadership to proclaim a yearly feast of celebration and remembrance.[2] This is the Jewish Festival of Lights, Hanukkah, (also celebrated in December). The New Testament refers to this feast as the Festival of Dedication (John 10:22).

As a result of the revolt, Israel was able to put their own Hasmonean Dynasty into power. However, it didn't last long. The Hasmoneans were overthrown by the Romans and oppression began anew. No king, no power, and no freedom were realities for God's people. To make matters worse, they were living in an age where God had suspended His revelation. For over 400 years, the people had received no prophetic word from the Lord. They were anxious to be free; the idea of a king who would be righteous and victorious sounded great to them. However, as usual, they missed the part about that king being humble and entering Jerusalem, not as a dominating force to deliver them from Rome, but as a servant.

Jesus fulfilled Zechariah's words on what we call Palm Sunday. He rode into Jerusalem on a donkey hailed as their King (Matthew 21:1-5; John 12:12-16). Little did they know, their King was going to Jerusalem to die and become the sacrifice that would completely fulfill their Scriptures.

---

[2] http://www.history.com/topics/holidays/hanukkah

In doing so, He would defeat an even greater enemy than Rome. Jesus' death and resurrection defeated Satan, the author of sin and death, and brought life and His own righteousness to all those (Jews or Gentiles) willing to accept His sacrifice on their behalf. That's a great reason to join with Zion in rejoicing!

The Old Testament prophets made little distinction between a first and second advent. The remainder of Zechariah's text speaks of the second advent of Christ when He comes as the conquering King who restores and renews Israel. God will be faithful to His promise to Israel—Christ will come again—and that is another reason to join with Zion in worship!

The Christmas season affords us many opportunities to rejoice and worship this King! We can worship through reading and studying his Word. We can worship through singing and offering praises and thanksgiving for the salvation and provision brought by the King. We can serve others as a representative of the King, and we can build His kingdom by telling others the good news. How can your family worship the King this Advent season?

> *Angels from the realms of glory*
> *Wing your flight o'er all the earth*
> *Ye who sang creation's story*
> *Now proclaim Messiah's birth*
>
> > *Come and worship*
> > *Come and worship*
> > *Worship Christ the new-born King*
>
> > > *Angels from the Realms of Glory*

Day 15 – God Works in the Waiting
Luke 1:5-13

⁵ In the time of Herod king of Judea there was a priest named Zechariah, who belonged to the priestly division of Abijah; his wife Elizabeth was also a descendant of Aaron. ⁶ Both of them were righteous in the sight of God, observing all the Lord's commands and decrees blamelessly. ⁷ But they were childless because Elizabeth was not able to conceive, and they were both very old.

⁸ Once when Zechariah's division was on duty and he was serving as priest before God, ⁹ he was chosen by lot, according to the custom of the priesthood, to go into the temple of the Lord and burn incense. ¹⁰ And when the time for the burning of incense came, all the assembled worshipers were praying outside.

¹¹ Then an angel of the Lord appeared to him, standing at the right side of the altar of incense. ¹² When Zechariah saw him, he was startled and was gripped with fear. ¹³ But the angel said to him: "Do not be afraid, Zechariah; your prayer has been heard. Your wife Elizabeth will bear you a son, and you are to call him John."

Zechariah (a different man than the prophet from yesterday's reading) was on temple duty. It was his job to keep the incense burning on the altar outside the Holy of Holies. This was a rare privilege. As duties were chosen by lot, many priests never had the opportunity to serve the Lord in this way. God used this very special moment in Zechariah's life to get his attention and build His kingdom through this upright man and his wife.

While Zechariah served in the temple, an angel of the Lord appeared to him with a startling announcement. "The prayer you've been praying since you and Elizabeth wed is going to be answered. You and your wife will have a son!" In this culture, being without children was often viewed very negatively. Being barren was seen by many as being under divine disfavor. This story is a near replica of the Lord's promise to Abram and his wife Sarai (Genesis 17:15-19) as well as Elkanah and his wife Hannah (1 Samuel 1:3-20). None of those stories had anything to do with disfavor from God either. In fact, the truth is quite the opposite. God chose people who loved and followed Him and allowed them to be vessels through which His glory flowed.

Zechariah and Elizabeth were to name their son John, which meant "the Lord is gracious." As you read the rest of this account, you will see that Zechariah realized the Lord was indeed gracious, though it was slow in coming by an earthly perspective. God's timing rarely seems to match up with our timing. However, as Zechariah and Elizabeth discovered, God is always on time. He is always searching for that special moment when He can display His glory in the lives of those who are committed to following Him.

Are you positioned to take hold of a divine moment? Zechariah and Elizabeth were probably devastated by their inability to conceive, but they didn't blame God or withhold their worship because they were upset that He wasn't answering their prayers how and when they wanted them answered.

Instead, they continued to believe, live holy lives, and position themselves in a place where God could work and show them His graciousness and glory.

We live in a world of instant gratification. We complain when the internet doesn't respond immediately; we complain when the drive-thru is too slow. We get bigger and more powerful microwaves, so we can have popcorn in ninety seconds instead of three minutes.

Elizabeth and Zechariah's story reminds us that God works in the waiting. He spent a lifetime preparing Zechariah for a single moment (Luke 1:18-20).

Christmas is all about waiting and expectation. We wait in lines at the stores. We wait for friends and family to visit. We wait to open gifts. Christmas, more than any other holiday, teaches us to wait.

For what are you waiting? Perhaps it's something big and God-sized like the child for which Zechariah and Elizabeth longed; perhaps it's an upcoming vacation or visit from someone special; perhaps it's just something small but important. Big or small, God wants us to wait with a heart that is committed to obedience and ready to receive.

Be still my soul, the Lord is on thy side
Bear patiently the cross of grief or pain
Leave to thy God to order and provide
In ev'ry change He faithful will remain
Be still my soul, thy best thy heav'nly Friend
Through thorny ways leads to a joyful end

Be Still My Soul

Day 16 – Time for a Change
Luke 1:14-17

14 *"He will be a joy and delight to you, and many will rejoice because of his birth,* 15 *for he will be great in the sight of the Lord. He is never to take wine or other fermented drink, and he will be filled with the Holy Spirit even before he is born.* 16 *He will bring back many of the people of Israel to the Lord their God.* 17 *And he will go on before the Lord, in the spirit and power of Elijah, to turn the hearts of the parents to their children and the disobedient to the wisdom of the righteous— to make ready a people prepared for the Lord."*

When Zechariah entered the temple to serve that day, he probably didn't expect to hear a direct word from the Lord. He definitely didn't expect God would answer his lifelong prayer, and he never would have dreamed he and Elizabeth would bear the child who would fulfill Isaiah's prophecy of a forerunner to the Messiah (Isaiah 40:3-5).

From birth, John would be a Nazarite (Judges 13:4-7; 1 Samuel 1:11). His life was committed to the service of God, and he was filled with the Spirit of God even before he was born. John was not Elijah come back to life, but a new prophet, like Elijah, who called people to repentance and back to true worship of God. He not only fulfilled Isaiah's prophecy, but a word from the book of Malachi as well:

> *5 "See, I will send the prophet Elijah to you before that great and dreadful day of the Lord comes. 6 He will turn the hearts of the parents to their children, and the hearts of the children to their parents."*
>
> *Malachi 4:5-6a*

Just like his parents were ready, John's job would be to get people ready for the coming of the Messiah. It had been over 400 years since a prophet of the Lord had delivered a message from God. It's easy to lose hope and lose focus when progress is slow or seemingly non-existent. But life was tough under Roman rule and Messianic hopes were high at the time of John's birth. John preached boldly and without compromise. His message of turning back to God was generally well received. Even Herod, though he'd arrested him after John condemned him for marrying his brother's wife, found John interesting and liked to listen to him preach (Matthew 14:1-11).

When most people think about John, they think about baptism. When a believer is submersed beneath the water in baptism, it symbolizes dying to the old self-directed life. When the believer emerges from the water, it symbolizes the beginnings of a new God-directed life. This is a picture of the repentance John preached. It is more than just being sorry; repentance is sorrow and change. When people have an encounter with God, real change should be the result.

In *The Best Christmas Pageant Ever*, we meet the Herdmans, a family of rough and tumble children who've never even heard, much less understood, the story of Christmas. Somehow, this motley crew manages to secure all the lead roles in the church Christmas pageant. As late as minutes before the show, they are still fighting, wrestling, and smoking cigars in the ladies' room. But then something happens... Imogene Herdman begins to understand who Jesus is, and we see a dramatic change in her behavior. Even Leroy, who is known for being a big bully, brings a ham from their welfare basket to give to the baby Jesus as the gift of the Magi. This boy, who has never given anything in his life, refuses to take the ham back after the pageant. The Herdman children encountered the Savior, and there was a genuine shift in how they thought and acted.[3]

God isn't an Elf on the Shelf or a Santa Claus in the sky, but He does watch us. He sees our actions and knows our secret thoughts (Psalm 139:1-4, 23-24). When we encounter God, we need to allow our lives to be changed by the power of His grace. That was John's message: "See God; see what He's doing in your world, repent, and change your behavior accordingly!" What is one change you could make today to bring your life more into alignment with God's standards?

---

[3] *The Best Christmas Pageant Ever,* Barbara Robinson. Harper and Row Publishers, New York, 1971.

When we walk with the Lord
In the light of His word
What a glory He sheds on our way
While we do His good will
He abides with us still
And with all who will trust and obey

Trust and obey
For there's no other way
To be happy in Jesus
But to trust and obey

Trust and Obey

Day 17 – The Struggle with Unbelief

Luke 1:18-25

18 Zechariah asked the angel, "How can I be sure of this? I am an old man and my wife is well along in years."

19 The angel said to him, "I am Gabriel. I stand in the presence of God, and I have been sent to speak to you and to tell you this good news. 20 And now you will be silent and not able to speak until the day this happens, because you did not believe my words, which will come true at their appointed time."

21 Meanwhile, the people were waiting for Zechariah and wondering why he stayed so long in the temple. 22 When he came out, he could not speak to them. They realized he had seen a vision in the temple, for he kept making signs to them but remained unable to speak.

23 When his time of service was completed, he returned home. 24 After this his wife Elizabeth became pregnant and for five months remained in seclusion. 25 "The Lord has done this for me," she said. "In these days he has shown his favor and taken away my disgrace among the people."

This short passage demonstrates the struggle between unbelief and faith. Zechariah questioned the angel, as anyone would have. He and Elizabeth had been trying to conceive for years and were unable. Finally, in their old age, God sent an angel to tell them they would have a baby? It sounded too good to be true, and Zechariah felt the need to confirm the angel's words. He probably didn't think the angel would "bless" him with muteness. His small measure of unbelief became a nine-month reminder of God's ability to do the impossible.

The other priests, levites, and worshippers waited outside the temple while Zechariah took hold of his divine moment. When he came out and could not speak, they realized he had heard from the Lord. Can you imagine how exciting that must have been? The Roman overlords were cruel and offensive to Jewish customs. The Romans kept the special garments worn by the High Priest during the festivals. The Jews had to receive permission from the government to celebrate their feasts and holy days. Things were hard, and the heavens had been silent for over four hundred years.

All of a sudden, God broke the silence with a message to Zechariah, "The Messiah is coming, and your son will go before Him!"

Zechariah finished his time of service and promptly returned home to put his faith in motion. He and Elizabeth conceived a child, and she spent five months waiting for confirmation. Elizabeth recognized what the Lord had done for her and was filled with joy!

Isn't this the story of life? We walk by faith until something difficult crosses our path. When we get squeezed, the unbelief comes pouring out and we question our divine appointments and our divine callings. Gideon, the leader of God's army against the Midianites, questioned his calling.

God had to prove his plan to Gideon through a series of tests before he was willing to leave the winepress where he was threshing wheat for fear of his enemies (Judges 6). Satan loves to work in seeds of doubt and unbelief. He planted the seed of doubt in Eve's mind, and the world was changed forever (Genesis 3:4-7).

This is why it is so important to study the character and work of God. God is faithful and unchanging (Malachi 3:6). He cannot do anything that is contrary to His Word or His nature. He saves in love, and He judges in love.

We must test the spirits to know whether or not they are from God (1 John 4:1). When teachings and advice align with the Word of God (His primary way of communicating with us), believe. When they do not align, then start to question. The angel's appearance to Zechariah was totally consistent with God's actions in the Hebrew Scriptures that Zechariah studied every day, yet his unbelief won the battle over his faith. We truly fight a spiritual battle (Ephesians 6:10-18).

We all struggle with doubts and unbelief from time to time. While our Christmas carols encourage us to "don our gay apparel," instead of ugly Christmas sweaters and light-up socks, put on the armor of God (Ephesians 6:14-17).

Which part of the armor (the belt of truth, the breastplate of righteousness, feet fitted with the readiness that comes from the gospel of peace, the shield of faith, the helmet of salvation, and the sword of the spirit) stands out as the most important piece in your personal journey with Jesus? This Christmas season you can overcome unbelief by being prepared to fight it.

'Tis so sweet to trust in Jesus
Just to take Him as His word
Just to rest upon His promise
Just to know thus saith the Lord

    Jesus, Jesus how I trust Him
    How I proved Him o'er and o'er
    Jesus, Jesus precious Jesus
    O for grace to trust Him more

        'Tis So Sweet to Trust in Jesus

Day 18 – God Chooses Mary
Luke 1:26-38

26 In the sixth month of Elizabeth's pregnancy, God sent the angel Gabriel to Nazareth, a town in Galilee, 27 to a virgin pledged to be married to a man named Joseph, a descendant of David. The virgin's name was Mary. 28 The angel went to her and said, "Greetings, you who are highly favored! The Lord is with you."

29 Mary was greatly troubled at his words and wondered what kind of greeting this might be. 30 But the angel said to her, "Do not be afraid, Mary; you have found favor with God. 31 You will conceive and give birth to a son, and you are to call him Jesus. 32 He will be great and will be called the Son of the Most High. The Lord God will give him the throne of his father David, 33 and he will reign over Jacob's descendants forever; his kingdom will never end."

34 "How will this be," Mary asked the angel, "since I am a virgin?"

35 The angel answered, "The Holy Spirit will come on you, and the power of the Most High will overshadow you. So the holy one to be born will be called the Son of God. 36 Even Elizabeth your relative is going to have a child in her old age, and she who was said to be unable to conceive is in her sixth month. 37 For no word from God will ever fail."

38 "I am the Lord's servant," Mary answered. "May your word to me be fulfilled." Then the angel left her.

Once again, the Lord chose an insignificant but godly individual to be a vessel for His glory. We don't know much about Mary other than her marital status. She was betrothed to Joseph in what was probably an arrangement between her father and his father. The two may have met, but it is unlikely she was marrying for love. We can imagine she was a typical Jewish girl, likely in her early teens. She was far too young for marriage and motherhood by today's standards, but it was normal for her culture. We know nothing of her family, though we can assume that they were God-honoring considering the favor God bestowed on their daughter. Many scholars believe Mary's genealogy is recorded in Luke 3; she was also from the family of David.

When the angel appeared, Mary, like everyone else who was blessed with an angelic appearance, was afraid. Gabriel reaffirmed God's favor on Mary before offering the life-changing announcement. This young lady, who had never been with a man, would conceive a child and name him Jesus. If that weren't enough, the angel went on to say that He would be called the Son of the Most High and that He would reign forever on the throne of His father David. Mary was going to be the mother of the Messiah the whole nation had been waiting for!

Mary questioned the angel; however, unlike her relative Zechariah who questioned, she didn't receive a consequence. Gabriel replied that the child conceived in her would come about by a miraculous work of the Holy Spirit. Though Joseph would be the child's earthly parent, he would not be the real father. God Himself would be the father. This made Jesus both God and man. This was very important to the plan of salvation since only a sinless sacrifice would be accepted as the payment for humanity's sins. Because all have sinned, a human alone couldn't atone (2 Corinthians 5:21; Romans 3:23). The angel also told Mary that her relative Elizabeth, who was considered barren, was in her sixth month of pregnancy.

Older translations render verse 37, "Nothing is impossible with God." The newer translations, in particular the NIV, state, "*No word from God will ever fail.*" While these two versions of the verse generally mean the same thing, the second rendering seems to confirm Mary's faith, as evidenced by the following verse. "*I am the Lord's servant… May your word to me be fulfilled.*" Mary believed God could and would do just as the angel said. She also believed God would protect her despite the risk.

Mary didn't understand how or why, but she was willing to participate in God's plan. She certainly knew the cost. She was not yet married; being with child out of wedlock was an offense punishable by stoning (Leviticus 20:10; John 8:3-5). Joseph would know the baby was not his child and would likely leave her (Matthew 1:18-19). But none of this was as important to Mary as submission to God.

How do you respond when God asks you to do something big or a little crazy for his kingdom? Would you tell the angel, "Forget it," or would you quietly and humbly acquiesce like Mary?

The good news is: God isn't going to ask you to carry His Son for nine months and bear Him outside of wedlock, but He does ask you to carry His Son in your lifestyle. Consider these instructions from the Apostle Paul:

> *We always carry around in our body the death of Jesus, so that the life of Jesus may also be revealed in our body.*
>
> *2 Corinthians 4:10*

> *I have been crucified with Christ and I no longer live, but Christ lives in me. The life I now live in the body, I live by faith in the Son of God, who loved me and gave himself for me.*
>
> *Galatians 2:20*

What is God asking of you this Christmas season? Does He want you to bake cookies, bring them to your neighbors, and invite them to a Christmas performance or service? (Or really go all out and share the gospel in their living room?) Does He want you to give up a present and instead use the money to bless someone less fortunate? Does He want you to serve in a soup kitchen or ring bells for the Salvation Army? Does He want you to stop bickering with your siblings or have a joyful attitude when visiting your in-laws on Christmas Day? Whatever He asks, how can you be the Lord's servant this Advent season?

> *Go, tell it on the mountain*
> *Over the hills and everywhere*
> *Go, tell it on the mountain*
> *That Jesus Christ is born*

Go Tell It on the Mountain

Day 19 – God with Us

Isaiah 7:10-14

¹⁰ Again the Lord spoke to Ahaz, ¹¹ "Ask the Lord your God for a sign, whether in the deepest depths or in the highest heights."

¹² But Ahaz said, "I will not ask; I will not put the Lord to the test."

¹³ Then Isaiah said, "Hear now, you house of David! Is it not enough to try the patience of humans? Will you try the patience of my God also? ¹⁴ Therefore the Lord himself will give you a sign: The virgin will conceive and give birth to a son and will call him Immanuel."

It was a darker time in Judah's history. Israel, its twin nation, formed a pact with Aram, an enemy nation, and they were setting out to destroy Judah. Through Isaiah, the Lord told King Ahaz of Judah not to be afraid. His enemies talked big and plotted big but in reality, were powerless and would be wiped out within sixty-five years (Isaiah 7:1-8). Israel's king, Pekah, was a usurper (someone who took the throne by force rather than right) and had no real claims to the throne and no chance to substantially challenge the Davidic king, Ahaz. Israel and Aram were ruled by human strength, but Judah was still ruled by the Lord. God would protect His own—of this, Ahaz could be certain.

God wanted Ahaz to trust that He would provide salvation, so instead of waiting for Ahaz to ask for a sign, as many are wont to do, God encouraged Ahaz to ask Him for a sign. But though Ahaz responded in a manner that appears humble, he was too proud to trust God. He wanted this deliverance to come from his own strength, so he declined God's gracious offer.

God had other plans; He chastised Ahaz for his pride and gave him a sign anyway. *The virgin will conceive and give birth to a son and will call Him Immanuel* (Isaiah 7:14). This prophecy is another one with double fulfillment. The Hebrew word used for virgin is *almah;* it refers to a woman about to be married. Many scholars believe this was Isaiah's second wife, the first having died in childbirth after the birth of his first son. Isaiah's second son, *Maher-Shalal-Hash-Baz,* was named significantly, "quick to the plunder." Before the boy was old enough to speak, Israel, at this point an enemy of Judah, was defeated and plundered by Assyria (722 BC). Israel no longer posed a threat to Ahaz or his kingdom (Isaiah 8:3-4). Because visions or signs were almost always fulfilled within a few years, most scholars believe Isaiah's son to be the initial fulfillment of this prophecy.

The name Immanuel (also correctly spelled Emmanuel) means "God with us," and was meant to assure Ahaz that he could trust God even though the situation looked bleak.

Many people also believe Immanuel was a second or complementary name for Maher-Shalal-Hash-Baz. God will protect his people by eventually destroying those who plot against them. (For another instance of a prophet's children having meaningful names, have a look at the book of Hosea. It is a beautiful story of God calling Israel back to Himself and protecting her though she was rather faithless).

We will see the second fulfillment of this prophecy in the angel's announcement to Joseph. Gospel writer, Matthew, understood this prophecy to ultimately speak of Jesus (Matthew 1:23).

For today, take some time to appreciate the idea of God being with us and in us.

When this prophecy was first given, the people could only relate to God through the mediation and intercession of a priest. Because of Jesus, you can go to God anytime and anywhere (Hebrews 4:14-16). In fact, Paul encourages believers to pray continually because your Heavenly Father is with you (1 Thessalonians 5:17). This passage also reminds us that God is faithful even when we are too proud or too afraid to trust Him. Sometimes, God works despite us. Thank God that through Jesus, we can approach Him with confidence knowing he forgives us and loves us.

> *O come, O come Emmanuel*
> *And ransom captive Israel*
> *Who mourns in lonely exile here*
> *Until the Son of God appear*
>
> > *Rejoice, rejoice*
> > *Emmanuel shall come to thee, O Israel*
>
> > > *O Come, O Come Emmanuel*

Day 20 – For Unto Us a Child is Born

Isaiah 9:2-7

2 The people walking in darkness
have seen a great light;
on those living in the land of deep darkness
a light has dawned.
³ You have enlarged the nation
and increased their joy;
they rejoice before you
as people rejoice at the harvest,
as warriors rejoice
when dividing the plunder.
⁴ For as in the day of Midian's defeat,
you have shattered
the yoke that burdens them,
the bar across their shoulders,
the rod of their oppressor.
⁵ Every warrior's boot used in battle
and every garment rolled in blood
will be destined for burning,
will be fuel for the fire.
⁶ For to us a child is born,
to us a son is given,
and the government will be on his shoulders.
And he will be called
Wonderful Counselor, Mighty God,
Everlasting Father, Prince of Peace.
⁷ Of the greatness of his government and peace
there will be no end.
He will reign on David's throne
and over his kingdom,
establishing and upholding it
with justice and righteousness
from that time on and forever.
The zeal of the Lord Almighty
will accomplish this.

Isaiah's words are some of the most beautiful and recognizable Messianic Scriptures. From thousands of choirs singing Handel's *Messiah,* to dozens of Christmas cards, these words are easily as popular as the nativity stories themselves.

The Messiah would be a great light in a very dark place. As in the days when God's small army, under Gideon's leadership, destroyed the Midianites (Judges 7:22-25), so will the present enemies of God (Assyria) and His people be destroyed. There will be no need for armies nor military equipment. God will be the deliverer.

Isaiah also affirms the other prophecies regarding the Messiah, mainly that He will be a world leader from the line of David. He will be great and powerful, and He will bring peace to the earth. John's prophecy in Revelation brings Isaiah's foreshadowing of a world of righteousness into greater focus as the millennial kingdom and the new Jerusalem are described (Revelation 20-21).

This passage also gives the reader an early glimpse into the nature of the promised Messiah. The Anointed One was more than just an outstanding human being. After all, Israel had some impressive kings. Saul was a physical specimen worth a second glance (1 Samuel 9:1-2). David was a mighty warrior and a king after God's own heart (1 Samuel 13:14). Solomon was wealthy and wise (1 Kings 3:12-13). But Isaiah uses four titles for this future King that are unlike Immanuel, which many scholars think is somewhat generic. These titles, more so than any other Old Testament references, point to the Messiah being not just *from* God, but God Himself.

Wonderful Counselor carries the idea of the Messianic King. In contrast to Ahaz, this new counselor would possess divine wisdom for leading the people. As the *Mighty God*, the Messiah would eventually bring about the end of the political and military challenges listed in verses 3-5, as well as all the other difficulties Israel faced being the chosen people of God. As the *Everlasting Father*, He would be worthy of trust as a compassionate, merciful provider and protector. As the *Prince of Peace*, He would finally bring all nations to an accord and institute peace on earth.

The Messiah is the end of the covenant promised to Abraham; He is the "seed" by which all nations will be blessed (Genesis 12:2-3; Galatians 3:15-16). He is also the end of the Davidic Covenant which placed a king in the line of David on the throne of Israel forever (2 Samuel 7:16). Isaiah's prophecy reminds us that God keeps His promises and is faithful to His covenants.

While these promises will ultimately be realized in the millennial kingdom, they are not without fulfillment today. Jesus the Messiah goes before us as our High Priest and makes intercession before God on our behalf (Romans 8:34). Because of this, God declares us justified—just as if we had never sinned (Romans 3:24). As the High Priest and the Messianic King, He opened the way for us to approach the throne of the *Wonderful Counselor*, the *Mighty God,* the *Everlasting Father,* and the *Prince of Peace* as often as we want with whatever concern we have (Hebrews 4:16). He gives us wisdom and insight in His Word (Hebrews 4:12). He fights our battles (Exodus 14:14). He tenderly provides for our needs (Philippians 4:19). And He gives us peace amid our anxiety (Philippians 4:6-7).

How has the Messiah been your *Wonderful Counselor, Mighty God, Everlasting Father*, and *Prince of Peace*?

For unto us a child is born
Unto us a son is given
Unto us a son is given

And the government shall be upon His shoulders
And the government shall be upon His shoulders
And His name shall be called

Wonderful Counselor
The Mighty God
The Everlasting Father
The Prince of Peace
The Everlasting Father
The Prince of Peace

For Unto Us a Child is Born

Day 21 – Elizabeth and Mary

Luke 1:39-45

39 At that time Mary got ready and hurried to a town in the hill country of Judea, 40 where she entered Zechariah's home and greeted Elizabeth. 41 When Elizabeth heard Mary's greeting, the baby leaped in her womb, and Elizabeth was filled with the Holy Spirit. 42 In a loud voice she exclaimed: "Blessed are you among women, and blessed is the child you will bear! 43 But why am I so favored, that the mother of my Lord should come to me? 44 As soon as the sound of your greeting reached my ears, the baby in my womb leaped for joy. 45 Blessed is she who has believed that the Lord would fulfill his promises to her!"

When this meeting occurred, Mary had already received her own angelic announcement. She set out with haste to visit with her relatives Zechariah and Elizabeth. Elizabeth was several months into her pregnancy by this point, and clearly, John was an active baby. He didn't just kick when Jesus showed up, he jumped! Luke tells us earlier that John would be filled with the Spirit even before birth, and this meeting gives evidence that, even in the womb, John was led by the Spirit and already making a way for the King (Luke 1:15). As he jumped, God's Spirit also came upon Elizabeth, and she proclaimed a blessing on Mary. We know Mary knew Elizabeth was with child (Luke 1:36), but the Scriptures don't tell us if Elizabeth knew the same of Mary, or if the Holy Spirit spoke this to her, and through her, in that very moment. What we do know is Elizabeth knew she was in the presence of the Lord. Her statement shows her great faith. She clearly understood the role her own son would play in preparing the way for the Messiah, and she also understood the importance of the child Mary carried.

Luke's gospel gives us four glimpses of godly men and women who were filled with the Spirit and recognized Mary's child as the Messiah (Luke 1:41-45; 2:21-38). These four, Elizabeth, Zechariah, Simeon, and Anna, come in stark contrast to the teachers of the law and the Pharisees, who knew the Hebrew Scriptures from years of study, but didn't really know the Lord and were not filled with the Holy Spirit. Because they weren't filled with the Spirit, their eyes were blinded when it came to Jesus, and instead of worshipping Him as God, they tested, falsely accused, and crucified Him. They took religion to an extreme and missed out on Jesus and the Holy Spirit.

This happens today as well. We love to celebrate Christmas, but we can easily become distracted by the holiday and forget the reason we're celebrating in the first place.

There is nothing wrong with decorating your home, baking some cookies, exchanging gifts, and watching Christmas movies on the Hallmark Channel. But when those things, rather than Jesus, become the focus and joy of the season, we've missed out, just like the Pharisees. Even the name Christmas (from Christ's Mass, a special worship service commemorating the birth of Christ), should remind us that it's all about Christ. And if that's not enough, consider the Spanish word *más* which ends our English word Christmas. This word means "more." (There is no actual grammatical connection in the word origin; we'll consider it a fortunate coincidence.) This Christmas, may you have MORE Christ. May your eyes, like Elizabeth's, be opened to the truth of the Lord and the Savior, and may you celebrate like John who jumped for joy in the presence of Jesus.

How can your family make Christmas MORE about Jesus this year?

O come all ye faithful, joyful and triumphant
O come ye, O come ye to Bethlehem
Come and behold Him
Born the King of angels

O come let us adore Him
O come let us adore Him
O come let us adore Him
Christ the Lord

O Come All Ye Faithful

Day 22 – The Magnificat

Luke 1:46-56

46 And Mary said:
"My soul glorifies the Lord
47   and my spirit rejoices in God my Savior,
48 for he has been mindful
*   of the humble state of his servant.*
From now on all generations will call me blessed,
49   for the Mighty One has done great things for me—
*   holy is his name.*
50 His mercy extends to those who fear him,
*   from generation to generation.*
51 He has performed mighty deeds with his arm;
*   he has scattered those who are proud in their inmost*
thoughts.
52 He has brought down rulers from their thrones
*   but has lifted up the humble.*
53 He has filled the hungry with good things
*   but has sent the rich away empty.*
54 He has helped his servant Israel,
*   remembering to be merciful*
55 to Abraham and his descendants forever,
*   just as he promised our ancestors."*
56 Mary stayed with Elizabeth for about three months and then
returned home.

M*ary Did You Know* is a popular Christmas song originally done by the Gaither Band. Its minor melody and unique harmonies are beautiful, not to mention fun to sing. Many groups, Christian artists and otherwise, have created their own rendition. But despite the beauty, the song questions things like: did Mary understand the boy would perform miracles; did she know He was God; did she know He was the Savior? These are not questions over which we should spend a lot of time pondering.

Newsflash, Mary knew! The answer to these questions is found in the Gospel of Luke, in Mary's own words. This passage, often called the *Magnificat,* is the first words of the song from the *Latin Vulgate*, a translation of the Bible completed by the church father Jerome around 400 AD. It is one of the four hymns of praise recorded in Luke 1-2 and is similar in nature to Hannah's song (1 Samuel 2:1-10).

Mary opens with a statement of exultation, "My soul, (*my inmost being, my thoughts, my emotions, and my will),* glorifies the Lord." Mary knew exactly what was happening. She knew the conception was a miracle. She knew the baby was God, and she knew He was the Messiah and the Savior!

Mary was amazed that God would favor her to be the mother of His Son. While we understand the expectancy of pregnancy and waiting for a child, we don't understand the level of expectancy Jewish women must have felt. Many a Jewish girl dreamed she would be the mother of the Messiah. When the angel announced the news to Mary, she was stunned, but she was ready to receive, and she knew where the glory belonged. Mary proclaimed the might, the mercy, the justice, the compassion, the provision, and the covenant faithfulness of God. Mary understood the program from the very beginning. Why else would she have responded to the angel with a such a gracious answer despite the stigma that would come from being with child out of wedlock?

This Christmas find a musical version of the *Magnificat* and rejoice with Mary in the knowledge that God knew what He was doing all along. He chose to send His salvation into the world through the borrowed womb of a teenage girl who was ready to receive the Son because she knew the Father. Do you know the Father? Are you ready to receive the Son?

> *Sing we now of Christmas*
> *Noel sing we here*
> *Listen to our praises*
> *To the Babe so dear*
>
> > *Sing we Noel*
> > *The King is born, Noel*
> > *Sing we now of Christmas*
> > *Sing we all Noel*

Sing We Now of Christmas

Day 23 – The Naming of John

Luke 1:57-66

57 *When it was time for Elizabeth to have her baby, she gave birth to a son.* **58** *Her neighbors and relatives heard that the Lord had shown her great mercy, and they shared her joy.* **59** *On the eighth day they came to circumcise the child, and they were going to name him after his father Zechariah,* **60** *but his mother spoke up and said, "No! He is to be called John."*

61 *They said to her, "There is no one among your relatives who has that name."*

62 *Then they made signs to his father, to find out what he would like to name the child.* **63** *He asked for a writing tablet, and to everyone's astonishment he wrote, "His name is John."*

64 *Immediately his mouth was opened and his tongue set free, and he began to speak, praising God.* **65** *All the neighbors were filled with awe, and throughout the hill country of Judea people were talking about all these things.* **66** *Everyone who heard this wondered about it, asking, "What then is this child going to be?" For the Lord's hand was with him.*

Since the time of Abraham, the people of God had been celebrating the covenant of circumcision and the naming of the child on the eighth day. God wanted His people to be set apart from the nations around them, so He gave them a covenant in the flesh that would brand them as His own. Just like ranchers and farmers mark their livestock as their own, God marked His people. Since Zechariah and Elizabeth were practicing Jews and devout followers of God, this ceremony of dedication, marking, and naming was especially important, and their family and friends gathered to celebrate with them.

It was custom during this time to give children a family name. In this instance, the crowd believed the boy should be named after his father, but Elizabeth was insistent he should be called John. The crowd groaned in reluctance and attempted to persuade her out of that choice by encouraging her to stick with tradition. But Elizabeth held her ground. She was so staunch in her stance on the boy's name that the crowd skirted around her and tried to persuade Zechariah by making signs to him. Apparently, they thought since he was unable to speak, he was also unable to hear. As God's Word only comments on Zechariah's loss of speech, we can assume the signs were unnecessary, but they do add a measure of humor to the scene as we picture a crowd of priests, family, and friends arguing with Zechariah through hand gestures.

As Zechariah was still unable to speak, he had to write the boy's name on a tablet for them. This act of faithful obedience loosened his tongue, and his first words in almost a year were praises for the God who had finally given him a child.
From birth, John had a reputation for being in the hand of the Lord. News didn't travel very quickly during those days, but word spread concerning John. No doubt this raised the Messianic expectation to fever pitch; the Lord was once again communicating with His people.

As we've seen, names in the Bible held a great deal of significance. John's name meant *the Lord is gracious.* Jesus and Joshua both mean *Yahweh is salvation* or *the Lord saves.* Do you know the meaning of your name and why you received it? Are you named for a family member? Were you named with a special prayer of dedication? If you don't know, find out, and perhaps make it a goal to live out the meaning of your name.

> *How great our joy (great our joy)*
> *Joy, joy, joy (joy, joy, joy)*
> *Praise we the Lord in heaven on high*
> *(Praise we the Lord in heaven on high)*

How Great Our Joy!

Day 24 – The Benedictus

Luke 1:67-80

⁶⁷ *His father Zechariah was filled with the Holy Spirit and prophesied:*
> ⁶⁸ *"Praise be to the Lord, the God of Israel,*
>   *because he has come to his people and redeemed them.*
> ⁶⁹ *He has raised up a horn of salvation for us*
>   *in the house of his servant David*
> ⁷⁰ *(as he said through his holy prophets of long ago),*
> ⁷¹ *salvation from our enemies*
>   *and from the hand of all who hate us—*
> ⁷² *to show mercy to our ancestors*
>   *and to remember his holy covenant,*
> ⁷³   *the oath he swore to our father Abraham:*
> ⁷⁴ *to rescue us from the hand of our enemies,*
>   *and to enable us to serve him without fear*
> ⁷⁵ *in holiness and righteousness before him all our days.*
> ⁷⁶ *And you, my child, will be called a prophet of the Most High;*
>   *for you will go on before the Lord to prepare the way for him,*
> ⁷⁷ *to give his people the knowledge of salvation*
>   *through the forgiveness of their sins,*
> ⁷⁸ *because of the tender mercy of our God,*
>   *by which the rising sun will come to us from heaven*
> ⁷⁹ *to shine on those living in darkness*
>   *and in the shadow of death,*
> *to guide our feet into the path of peace."*

⁸⁰ *And the child grew and became strong in spirit; and he lived in the wilderness until he appeared publicly to Israel.*

Zechariah was filled with the Spirit and spoke in words of worship and prophecy. Mary knew; so did Zechariah. This family understood its role in God's redemptive plan!
This passage, known as the *Benedictus*, is also titled from the Latin Vulgate. It is ironic that when Zechariah finished his service in the temple, he was supposed to come out and pronounce a benediction, a closing blessing, a *benedictus,* on the people. However, when he finished, he was unable to speak. It is very fitting that when his speech returned, his first words were this Spirit-inspired blessing. It is filled with quotations from the Hebrew Scriptures relating the births of John and Jesus to prophecies concerning the Messiah and His forerunner.

One might think a new father, especially one who had been waiting decades to become so, would begin his soliloquy with an exultation concerning his own son. But Zechariah's first words spoke of the One who would be greater than his own son. "He has raised up a *horn of salvation* for us in the house of His servant David." Zechariah's words tied the coming Messiah to the Davidic Covenant (2 Samuel 7:11b-16). The term *horn of salvation* was a common expression in the Hebrew Scriptures. It was a symbol of strength (Deuteronomy 33:17), of God's mighty arm of salvation for the people. Mary also refers to the strength of God for salvation in her hymn of praise (Luke 1:51). If the Jewish people knew one thing about the character of God, it was that He was *strong to save*. His deliverance of the people from slavery in Egypt and the surrounding miracles were regularly rehearsed in their worship (Psalm 136, among other places). Throughout Israel's history, God painted pictures of the salvation that would someday come through His Son.

After Zechariah ties the promised Messiah to the Davidic Covenant, he also ties Him to the Abrahamic Covenant (Genesis 12:1-3; 15:18-21) indicating that salvation would come as a gift from God—grace, not works (Ephesians 2:8-9). At the time God called Abram, he had done nothing to deserve salvation, but God chose him and gifted him anyway.

Zechariah's words show an amazing understanding of who the Messiah would be. He would bring eternal salvation, but He would also give us a sin-forgiven righteousness. This righteousness allows us to approach the Father without fear because God's law is now written on our hearts (John 16:23-24). This is part of what scholars call the New Covenant which was given through the prophet Jeremiah:

> *31 "The days are coming," declares the Lord,*
> *   "when I will make a new covenant*
> *with the people of Israel*
> *   and with the people of Judah.*
> *32 It will not be like the covenant*
> *   I made with their ancestors*
> *when I took them by the hand*
> *   to lead them out of Egypt,*
> *because they broke my covenant,*
> *   though I was a husband to them,"*
> *declares the Lord.*
> *33 "This is the covenant I will make with the people of Israel*
> *   after that time," declares the Lord.*
> *"I will put my law in their minds*
> *   and write it on their hearts.*
> *I will be their God,*
> *   and they will be my people.*
> *34 No longer will they teach their neighbor,*
> *   or say to one another, 'Know the Lord,'*
> *because they will all know me,*
> *   from the least of them to the greatest,"*
> *declares the Lord.*
> *"For I will forgive their wickedness*
> *   and will remember their sins no more."*

Jeremiah 31:31-34

Zechariah understood the godship and the personhood of the Messiah, but he also understood the role his own son would play. Zechariah knew his son would function as the prophet who paved the way for the coming of the King (Isaiah 40:3-5; Malachi 4:5-6). His ministry would call the people to turn back to God and soften their hearts to receive salvation.

For hundreds of years, the people of God had been setting an extra cup at the *seder* (the Passover meal) for Elijah, the forerunner to the Messiah.[4] John is linked to Elijah throughout the gospel accounts, though some argue that he is not the forerunner because he said he wasn't Elijah (John 1:21). Sin blinded the people's eyes from being able to see that while John was not a reincarnated Elijah, he did come in the spirit and ministry style of Elijah (Luke 1:17; Matthew 3:1-4; 14:3). As Elijah pointed the people to the power and salvation of Yahweh during the reigns of Ahab and Jezebel, so John pointed the people to the power and salvation of Jesus. The tradition of *Elijah's Cup* was fulfilled in the person of John, but many well-meaning and God-fearing Jews didn't see it.

John's ministry was about preparation. Christmas is the holiday for which we seem to spend the most time preparing. We spend hours picking and trimming a tree, baking cookies and goodies, purchasing and wrapping gifts, and preparing our homes and lives to celebrate. There is nothing wrong with these preparations unless they, rather than the Savior, become the celebration. We need to spend time preparing our hearts to receive Jesus by being in His Word, by seeking Him through prayer, by remembering His salvation through worship (privately and with others), and by giving what we have received to a world desperately in need of the hope He brings.

Are you ready for the Messiah? Have you spent as much time preparing your heart as you've spent preparing your home? Today, set aside some time to worship like Zechariah did.

---

4   http://www.jewishanswers.org/ask-the-rabbi-category/the-jewish-calendar-and-holidays/passover/page/4/?p=1178

Good Christian men rejoice
With heart and soul and voice
Give ye heed to what we say
News, news, Jesus Christ is born today
Ox and ass before Him bow
And He is in the manger now
Christ is born today, Christ is born today

Good Christian men rejoice
With heart and soul and voice
Now ye hear of endless bliss
Jesus Christ was born for this
He has opened heaven's door
And man is blessed forevermore
Christ is born today, Christ is born today

Good Christian men rejoice
With heart and soul and voice
Now ye need not fear the grave
Jesus Christ was born to save
Calls you one and calls you all
To gain His everlasting hall
Christ was born to save, Christ was born to save

Good Christian Men Rejoice

Day 25 – An Angel Appears to Joseph

Matthew 1:18-25

18 *This is how the birth of Jesus the Messiah came about: His mother Mary was pledged to be married to Joseph, but before they came together, she was found to be pregnant through the Holy Spirit.* **19** *Because Joseph her husband was faithful to the law, and yet did not want to expose her to public disgrace, he had in mind to divorce her quietly.*

20 *But after he had considered this, an angel of the Lord appeared to him in a dream and said, "Joseph son of David, do not be afraid to take Mary home as your wife, because what is conceived in her is from the Holy Spirit.* **21** *She will give birth to a son, and you are to give him the name Jesus, because he will save his people from their sins."*

22 *All this took place to fulfill what the Lord had said through the prophet:* **23** *"The virgin will conceive and give birth to a son, and they will call him Immanuel" (which means "God with us").*

24 *When Joseph woke up, he did what the angel of the Lord had commanded him and took Mary home as his wife.* **25** *But he did not consummate their marriage until she gave birth to a son. And he gave him the name Jesus.*

The Scriptures are rather mum about Joseph apart from this passage and a few others in which Matthew takes care to let his readers know Joseph was also a godly individual. After all, he was chosen to be the earthly father to God.

Jewish law was very strict when it came to women being with child outside of wedlock (Leviticus 20:10), but it was much more lenient when it came to the man's role in a divorce. There were some leaders, from the Hillel school of thought, who were in favor of "no fault" divorce. This leniency meant that a man could divorce his wife for anything from burning the meatloaf to displeasing him in any way (Matthew 19:3). We know from Joseph's actions that he wasn't subscribing to the dilution of God's standards being preached by some of the religious leaders of his day.

By Mosaic law, Joseph could separate from his betrothed or his spouse if he found her to have compromised her purity (Deuteronomy 24:1). It was under this standard Joseph planned to break his covenant with Mary, though he planned to do so in such a way that she would not be publicly shamed. (See, he really was a decent guy even though he wasn't the star of the Christmas show.)

But God had bigger plans for Joseph. And He sent another angel, this time in a dream, to let him in on God's plan to bring salvation through the womb of his betrothed and through his family. Matthew, who was writing to his fellow Jews attempting to prove Jesus of Nazareth was the fulfillment of their Scriptures concerning the Messiah, ties the angel's announcement to the prophecy to King Ahaz:

> *"The virgin will conceive and give birth to a son and will call him Immanuel."*

> *Isaiah 7:14*

We continue to see Joseph's godly heart when he wakes from his dream. He didn't hesitate, he didn't run away, he didn't try to make it look different from reality by telling half-truths; he just obeyed and took Mary to be his wife. He sacrificed his rights to be angry about his circumstances and separate from something that appeared to be wrong. He honored the work God was doing through his betrothed even though it brought disgrace on him as well.

Sometimes God asks us to do hard things that are uncomfortable and inconvenient. Both Mary and Joseph willingly accepted the challenge and responsibility God gave them. They are examples of humble submission to the will of God. They were a poor couple who didn't have much to offer. But instead of choosing the wealthy and learned, God chose the humble and simple because they were willing to trust He had a plan even when they couldn't see it.

God wants hearts that are committed to trusting Him in the big and in the small. How has God asked you to trust Him? Does he want you to trust Him through a health crisis? Does He want you to trust Him through financial struggles? Does He want you to trust Him through relational difficulties? Does He want you to trust Him for an uncertain future?

God is wholly sovereign and completely worthy of our trust.

> [11] *"For I know the plans I have for you," declares the Lord, "plans to prosper you and not to harm you, plans to give you hope and a future.* [12] *Then you will call on me and come and pray to me, and I will listen to you.* [13] *You will seek me and find me when you seek me with all your heart."*
>
> Jeremiah 29:11-13

The same God who was faithful to Joseph will be faithful to you when you trust and obey.

How firm a foundation, ye saints of the Lord
Is laid for your faith in His excellent word
What more can He say than to you He hath said
To you whom for refuge to Jesus have fled

Fear not I am with thee, O be not dismayed
For I am thy God and will still give thee aid
I'll strengthen thee, help thee, and cause thee to stand
Upheld by my righteous omnipotent hand

When through fiery trials thy pathways shall lie
My grace all sufficient shall be thy supply
The flames shall not hurt thee I only design
Thy dross to consume and thy gold to refine

The soul that on Jesus hath leaned for repose
I will not, I will not desert to its foes
The soul though all hell should endeavor to shake
I'll never, no never, no never forsake

How Firm a Foundation

Day 26 – The Birth of Jesus
Luke 2:1-7

1 In those days Caesar Augustus issued a decree that a census should be taken of the entire Roman world. 2 (This was the first census that took place while Quirinius was governor of Syria.) 3 And everyone went to their own town to register.

4 So Joseph also went up from the town of Nazareth in Galilee to Judea, to Bethlehem the town of David, because he belonged to the house and line of David. 5 He went there to register with Mary, who was pledged to be married to him and was expecting a child. 6 While they were there, the time came for the baby to be born, 7 and she gave birth to her firstborn, a son. She wrapped him in cloths and placed him in a manger, because there was no guest room available for them.

Historical records show that censuses which required all persons to report to the place of their birth were regular customs in the ancient world. When Caesar Augustus issued this decree, it was probably seen as a hardship because of the foot travel involved, but it wasn't anything out of the ordinary. Since families generally had a substantial period in which to complete the registry process, those having to travel had time to plan for a lengthy journey.

Each year, the Jews celebrated three feasts which were considered pilgrimage feasts. The first of these feasts was Passover, which occurred in March or April. The second pilgrimage feast was *Shavuot*, the Feast of Weeks, (also known as Pentecost), which was celebrated fifty days after Passover. The final feast was *Sukkot*, the Feast of Tabernacles, which was celebrated in September or October.[5] All Jewish males were to appear before the Lord at a place appointed for the celebration (by Joseph's time, this was Jerusalem) to celebrate each of these feasts (Deuteronomy 16:16). Since Joseph's current home of Nazareth was a significant distance north of Jerusalem, it is likely the couple combined their duties to Rome with their pilgrimage to Passover. Perhaps you have traveled a few miles out of the way to visit friends or family on your road trip to Disney World or another vacation destination. Even with much faster ways of conveyance, we still make as few trips as possible.

Upon arrival in Bethlehem, they found no place to stay. This is rather significant since they were returning to Joseph's ancestral home where there likely would have been relatives. One can see the shunning the couple received from their own family who did not have the same understanding of God's plan as they did.

---

[5] For an excellent look at Jesus in the Jewish feasts check out *Celebrating Jesus in the Biblical Feasts*, Richard Booker. Destiny Image Publishers, Shippensburg, PA, 2008.

Instead of bedding down with relations, Mary and Joseph were forced to find accommodations elsewhere and sought to find a room at a local inn where they were told there was no vacancy.

We can almost picture the innkeeper's concern and embarrassment as he gives the couple the only thing he has a to offer, a shelter where he keeps his animals. It's rather fitting, don't you think? The Lamb of God, born in a barn… These verses remind us of the popular Christmas song, *The Little Drummer Boy (*Katherine Kennicott Davis, 1941). Like the boy in the story, the innkeeper had little to offer Jesus, but he gave what he could.

This Christmas may find you in a place like the inn keeper or the Little Drummer Boy. They had little in terms of worldly significance to offer Jesus, but they gave what they could. What is your stable, your song, or your small gift of love? What can you bring to Jesus this Christmas season?

> *What can I give Him, poor as I am*
> *If I were a shepherd, I would bring a lamb*
> *If I were a wise man, I would do my part*
> *Yet what can I give Him*
> *Give Him my heart*

> *What Can I Give Him?*

Day 27 – Hurry Shepherds, Run!

Luke 2:8-20

8 And there were shepherds living out in the fields nearby, keeping watch over their flocks at night. 9 An angel of the Lord appeared to them, and the glory of the Lord shone around them, and they were terrified. 10 But the angel said to them, "Do not be afraid. I bring you good news that will cause great joy for all the people. 11 Today in the town of David a Savior has been born to you; he is the Messiah, the Lord. 12 This will be a sign to you: You will find a baby wrapped in cloths and lying in a manger."

13 Suddenly a great company of the heavenly host appeared with the angel, praising God and saying,
14 "Glory to God in the highest heaven,
and on earth peace to those on whom his favor rests."

15 When the angels had left them and gone into heaven, the shepherds said to one another, "Let's go to Bethlehem and see this thing that has happened, which the Lord has told us about."

16 So they hurried off and found Mary and Joseph, and the baby, who was lying in the manger. 17 When they had seen him, they spread the word concerning what had been told them about this child, 18 and all who heard it were amazed at what the shepherds said to them. 19 But Mary treasured up all these things and pondered them in her heart. 20 The shepherds returned, glorifying and praising God for all the things they had heard and seen, which were just as they had been told.

When we reflect on this event after the fact, the Lamb of God being born in a barn makes perfect sense. The angelic announcement of the birth of the Lamb, during lambing season, to a group of shepherds, also makes perfect sense.

Likewise, the shepherd's response is worth noting. Though they initially responded to the angel with fear and awe, the shepherds didn't need to be told twice. They immediately left their flocks in the field and went to Bethlehem to worship. They were so moved by the announcement and their encounter with the couple and their child, they couldn't stop talking about their experience in the ensuing days. One can picture a group of stinky shepherds-turned-town-criers, running through the streets of Bethlehem telling everyone the good news of the birth of God's Son.

This was a special moment of confirmation for Mary. She must have known that, though she had endured great emotional suffering from her family and friends, she had done the right thing to accept the Lord's favor and carry His Son. One can imagine the joy she must have felt holding the tiny baby in her arms, stroking His soft velvety head, and rocking Him to sleep. One can also imagine the reverent fear she must have experienced in knowing the child she was holding was not just her own flesh and blood but God.

The story of Jesus' birth is convincing proof of the sovereignty and plan of God the Father. Though the details of the birth of the King seem unconventional, and probably not how we would have done it, God's plan was too crazy and detailed to be coincidence. This moment in history was planned from the beginning of time. As you celebrate Christ's birth, take time to join with the angels and the shepherds in giving glory to God for His sovereignty.

Hark the herald angels sing
Glory to the newborn King
Peace on earth and mercy mild
God and sinners reconciled
Joyful all ye nations rise
Join the triumph of the skies
With angelic host proclaim
Christ is born in Bethlehem
Hark the herald angels sing
Glory to the newborn King

Christ by highest heaven adored
Christ the Everlasting Lord
Late in time behold Him come
Offspring of the virgin's womb
Veiled in flesh the Godhead see
Hail the Incarnate Deity
Pleased as man with man to dwell
Jesus our Emmanuel
Hark the herald angels sing
Glory to the newborn King

Hail the Heaven-born Prince of Peace
Hail the Sun of Righteousness
Light and life to all He brings
Risen with healing in his wings
Mild He lays His glory by
Born that man no more may die
Born to save the sons of earth
Born to give them second birth
Hark the herald angels sing
Glory to the newborn King

Hark! The Herald Angels Sing

Day 28 – Simeon Blesses the Baby

Luke 2:21-35

21 *On the eighth day, when it was time to circumcise the child, he was named Jesus, the name the angel had given him before he was conceived.*

22 *When the time came for the purification rites required by the Law of Moses, Joseph and Mary took him to Jerusalem to present him to the Lord* **23** *(as it is written in the Law of the Lord, "Every firstborn male is to be consecrated to the Lord),* **24** *and to offer a sacrifice in keeping with what is said in the Law of the Lord: "a pair of doves or two young pigeons."*

25 *Now there was a man in Jerusalem called Simeon, who was righteous and devout. He was waiting for the consolation of Israel, and the Holy Spirit was on him.* **26** *It had been revealed to him by the Holy Spirit that he would not die before he had seen the Lord's Messiah.* **27** *Moved by the Spirit, he went into the temple courts. When the parents brought in the child Jesus to do for him what the custom of the Law required,* **28** *Simeon took him in his arms and praised God, saying:*

> **29** *"Sovereign Lord, as you have promised,*
> *   you may now dismiss your servant in peace.*
> **30** *For my eyes have seen your salvation,*
> **31** *which you have prepared in the sight of all nations:*
> **32** *a light for revelation to the Gentiles,*
> *   and the glory of your people Israel."*

33 *The child's father and mother marveled at what was said about him.* **34** *Then Simeon blessed them and said to Mary, his mother: "This child is destined to cause the falling and rising of many in Israel, and to be a sign that will be spoken against,* **35** *so that the thoughts of many hearts will be revealed. And a sword will pierce your own soul too."*

Simeon was an old man who had been waiting and longing for the Messiah for many years. The Holy Spirit promised him he would not die until he saw the salvation of the Lord in person. When Joseph and Mary brought their baby to the temple for His dedication, the Spirit moved Simeon, and he went to the temple too. He knew the pair of young people before him was no ordinary couple and the child no ordinary baby. He must have been a sight to see. It's likely he hadn't moved anywhere quickly in years, but one can imagine him hustling his ancient frame up to the couple to catch a glimpse of their child. One wonders if they reluctantly surrendered Him to Simeon's arms. They were not from Jerusalem; they wouldn't have recognized the old man. They probably thought he was crazy.

But Joseph and Mary had been obedient to the Spirit's leading all along, so why would that day be any different? Mary extended the child to Simeon, who cradled Him in his arms and began to praise the Lord for His salvation. Simeon knew the little one he held was the Messiah. He understood the baby was God's salvation wrapped in wrinkly skin and soft fuzzy hair. He beheld the *Wonderful Counselor*, the *Mighty God*, the *Everlasting Father*, and the *Prince of Peace*. He knew the child was the glory of Israel, but He would not just be salvation for God's people alone; He would bring reconciliation and redemption to all people.

Simeon likewise understood the child would be rejected and He would cause much disruption amongst His own people. He even warned Mary her heart would someday break over her child. Simeon clearly understood Isaiah's words spoken of the child in his arms:

> *¹ Who has believed our message*
> *and to whom has the arm of the Lord been revealed?*
> *² He grew up before him like a tender shoot,*
> *and like a root out of dry ground.*
> *He had no beauty or majesty to attract us to him,*

nothing in his appearance that we should desire
him.
³ He was despised and rejected by mankind,
  a man of suffering, and familiar with pain.
Like one from whom people hide their faces
  he was despised, and we held him in low esteem.
⁴ Surely he took up our pain
  and bore our suffering,
yet we considered him punished by God,
  stricken by him, and afflicted.
⁵ But he was pierced for our transgressions,
  he was crushed for our iniquities;
the punishment that brought us peace was on him,
  and by his wounds we are healed.
⁶ We all, like sheep, have gone astray,
  each of us has turned to our own way;
and the Lord has laid on him
  the iniquity of us all.

Isaiah 53:1-6

Mary knew, Joseph knew, and Simeon knew. The Spirit of God was already active in the lives of those who were devoted to following the Lord. Their actions and speech gave evidence of their faith in God. If you are a follower of Christ, there should be evidence in your life. Paul teaches the church in Galatia that the Holy Spirit produces fruit in the life of a believer. Love, joy, peace, patience, kindness, goodness, faithfulness, gentleness, and self-control (Galatians 5:22-23) are just a few evidences of the Spirit-filled life. Simeon waited patiently filled with the peace that God would keep His promise. How are you displaying these proofs of the Spirit in your life?

Come Thou long expected Jesus
Born to set Thy people free
From our fears and sins release us
Let us find our rest in Thee
Israel's strength and consolation
Hope of all the earth Thou art
Dear desire of every nation
Joy of every longing heart

Born Thy people to deliver
Born a child and yet a King
Born to reign in us forever
Now Thy gracious kingdom bring
By Thy own eternal Spirit
Rule in all our hearts alone
By Thine all sufficient merit
Raise us to Thy glorious throne.

Jesus what a friend for sinners
Jesus lover of my soul
Friends may fail me, foes assail me
He my Savior makes me whole
Hallelujah, what a Savior
Hallelujah, what a Friend
Saving, helping, keeping, loving
He is with me to the end

Come Thou Long Expected Jesus
Jesus What a Friend for Sinners

Day 29 – The Visit of the Magi

Matthew 2:1-12

1 *After Jesus was born in Bethlehem in Judea, during the time of King Herod, Magi from the east came to Jerusalem* **2** *and asked, "Where is the one who has been born king of the Jews? We saw his star when it rose and have come to worship him."*

3 *When King Herod heard this he was disturbed, and all Jerusalem with him.* **4** *When he had called together all the people's chief priests and teachers of the law, he asked them where the Messiah was to be born.* **5** *"In Bethlehem in Judea,"* *they replied, "for this is what the prophet has written:*

6 *"'But you, Bethlehem, in the land of Judah,*
are by no means least among the rulers of Judah;
for out of you will come a ruler
who will shepherd my people Israel."

7 *Then Herod called the Magi secretly and found out from them the exact time the star had appeared.* **8** *He sent them to Bethlehem and said, "Go and search carefully for the child. As soon as you find him, report to me, so that I too may go and worship him."*

9 *After they had heard the king, they went on their way, and the star they had seen when it rose went ahead of them until it stopped over the place where the child was.* **10** *When they saw the star, they were overjoyed.* **11** *On coming to the house, they saw the child with his mother Mary, and they bowed down and worshiped him. Then they opened their treasures and presented him with gifts of gold, frankincense and myrrh.* **12** *And having been warned in a dream not to go back to Herod, they returned to their country by another route.*

The birth of a new king was significant enough to draw the attention of learners from the East. Many scholars believe these Magi, or wise men, were residents in Babylon or Persia and were perhaps associated with the same schools as Daniel. We know they were interested in astronomy because they clearly noticed signs in the stars they found remarkable. Christian tradition generally holds there were three Magi because there were three gifts, but it is certainly possible that more than just three men made the lengthy journey to discover who they believed was a new king.[6]

Upon arrival in Jerusalem, they made their way to Herod's palace and inquired of the new king. Herod's peaceful existence was disrupted by the news, so he summoned his intelligence, as well as the Jewish leaders, to find out what was prophesied about this "so-called king." He was given the birth prophecy from Micah indicating the child would be born in Bethlehem (Micah 5:2). He sent for the Magi and ordered them to return to him after they found the child (in other words... did all the grunt work for him), so he could also go to worship.

Still following the star, the Magi made their way south of Jerusalem to Bethlehem where the star stopped over the house in which the child was living. The Scriptures use the Greek word *paidion* to describe the child. This word is used in reference to toddlers rather than little babies.

---

[6] For some interesting science that corroborates the Biblical facts presented in Matthew with regards to the star, check out bethlehemstar.com or view the DVD *The Star of Bethlehem.* Rick Larson (Christian, lawyer, and astronomical enthusiast) began to wonder if science backed up the Biblical account of the star. With the technology available to us today, Larson was able to trace exactly what was happening with the orbits of the planets and stars around the time of Christ's birth and how they pointed to a King in Judah.

Contrary to every nativity set in the world, the Wise Men did not show up at the manger but rather at a small house in Bethlehem. When the Magi reached the place where the child and His family lived, they presented Him with three symbolic gifts: gold, frankincense, and myrrh. The more obscure verses of *We Three Kings* tell the story of the gifts: gold for a king, incense for a God, and myrrh, a burial spice, for a sacrifice.

How did these Magi interpret the signs so correctly? How did they know what gifts to bring? Some suggest they were Jews still living in Babylon after the return from exile. Perhaps they knew and understood the prophecies concerning the Messiah. Regardless, these men—pagan kings, astrologers, Zoroastrians, Jews, or whoever they were—were inspired by the Holy Spirit and were obedient to His leading to follow and worship.

This is significant because it sets the tone for our response to the Holy Spirit and the birth of the King. It's very easy to keep Jesus in a manger where He is cute, cuddly, and under our control. But the reality is, Jesus is the King, He is God, and He is the High Priest whose sacrifice covered over and removed our sins. Because of those three truths, Jesus commands our belief, our worship, and our obedience. Anything less is an offense to the Godhead.

Baby Jesus in a manger is a lovely thought, but following God is so much more than just celebrating Christmas. It's about denying our self-serving desires, putting others before ourselves, giving generously, obeying even when it's not easy or convenient, and the list could go on. How can you get Jesus out of the manger and into your everyday life as the reigning King?

Born a babe on Bethlehem's plain
Gold I bring to crown Him again
King forever ceasing never
Over us all to reign

Frankincense to offer have I
Incense owns a Deity night
Prayer and praising all men raising
Worship Him God on high

Myrrh is mine its bitter perfume
Breathes a life of gathering doom
Suffering, sighing, bleeding, dying
Sealed in a stone-cold tomb

Glorious now behold Him arise
King and God and sacrifice
Alleluia, alleluia
Sounds through the earth and skies

We Three Kings

Day 30 – Out of Egypt

Matthew 2:13-23

13 *When they had gone, an angel of the Lord appeared to Joseph in a dream. "Get up," he said, "take the child and his mother and escape to Egypt. Stay there until I tell you, for Herod is going to search for the child to kill him."*

14 *So he got up, took the child and his mother during the night and left for Egypt,* **15** *where he stayed until the death of Herod. And so was fulfilled what the Lord had said through the prophet: "Out of Egypt I called my son."*

16 *When Herod realized that he had been outwitted by the Magi, he was furious, and he gave orders to kill all the boys in Bethlehem and its vicinity who were two years old and under, in accordance with the time he had learned from the Magi.* **17** *Then what was said through the prophet Jeremiah was fulfilled:*

> **18** *"A voice is heard in Ramah,*
> *weeping and great mourning,*
> *Rachel weeping for her children*
> *and refusing to be comforted,*
> *because they are no more."*

19 *After Herod died, an angel of the Lord appeared in a dream to Joseph in Egypt* **20** *and said, "Get up, take the child and his mother and go to the land of Israel, for those who were trying to take the child's life are dead."*

21 *So he got up, took the child and his mother and went to the land of Israel.* **22** *But when he heard that Archelaus was reigning in Judea in place of his father Herod, he was afraid to go there. Having been warned in a dream, he withdrew to the district of Galilee,* **23** *and he went and lived in a town called Nazareth. So was fulfilled what was said through the prophets, that he would be called a Nazarene.*

*A*fter the departure of the Magi, the angel of the Lord again appeared to Joseph in a dream instructing Him to flee to Egypt and stay there until the Lord allowed Him to return to Nazareth. Over the last couple of years, Joseph's life had been filled with angelic messages and crazy expectations, so he didn't think twice or even delay his flight until morning. They got up and left immediately. Matthew ties this escape to Egypt to Hosea's prophecy (Hosea 11:1). God had already called His people out of Egypt once; why not do it a second time? Certainly, Matthew saw the history of Israel being repeated in the early life of Jesus.

When Herod realized the Magi weren't coming back, he took matters into his own hands and ordered all boys in Bethlehem and the surrounding countryside who were two years old and younger to be put to death. Killing innocents was very much in line with Herod's typical actions. Rumors state he killed his own son because he thought he posed a threat to the throne. This order mirrors a similar command from another wicked ruler who was attempting to wipe out God's plan of salvation when the patriarch Moses when was born. The escape from Egypt during Moses' time was a preview of the salvation brought by Jesus (Exodus 1-14). Remember, Moses is a "type" of Christ.

Matthew also ties this massacre, small but brutal, to Jeremiah's prophecy about Rachel, Jacob's wife (a metaphor for Israel), weeping as her children passed through the city of Ramah on their way to exile in Babylon (Jeremiah 31:15). There will always be sin and evil in the world, but evil will not overcome God. God will protect His own. This doesn't mean that no harm will ever befall people who love and obey God, but there will always be purpose and plan in the troubles of this life (Romans 8:28).

After Herod died, another angel appeared to Joseph to let him know it was safe to return to Judea.

The new ruler wasn't a huge improvement on Herod, so yet another angel warned him to move back to Nazareth in Galilee rather than returning to his ancestral home of Bethlehem (which was only seven miles south of Jerusalem and a bit too close for comfort). The family resettled in Nazareth, which was well north of Jerusalem. We have reason to believe Jesus called Nazareth His home until He began his public ministry around the age of thirty.

Jesus' first advent was all about being a humble servant. He was born in a barn; His birth was witnessed by smelly animals and even smellier shepherds. Many people missed His first advent because they were so focused on the prophecies concerning His second advent when He will return to earth as the conquering King. They forgot that their hero, King David, was a shepherd before he became a King; the Son of David was also a shepherd before becoming a King.

This Christmas don't miss the moments and the opportunities God has given you because you're so focused on what you want to be or think you should be. The Hebrew people have suffered without their Messiah for the past two thousand years; they missed seeing Jesus as the glue that held together the whole mosaic of redemption. He didn't come into the world as the superhero for whom they were waiting, and Israel missed its moment.

Zechariah didn't miss his moment. Mary didn't miss her moment. Joseph didn't miss his moment. Simeon didn't miss his either. Open your eyes, open your ears, open your heart, and don't miss your moment!

Hallelujah
For the Lord God omnipotent reigneth
Hallelujah
The kingdom of this world is become
The Kingdom of our Lord and of His Christ
And of His Christ
And He shall reign forever and ever
Hallelujah

Hallelujah Chorus

God's Plan of Salvation

All humanity is guilty of sin and rejecting God (Romans 3:23). A basic definition for sin is *loving yourself more than you love God*. God specifically listed ten offenses to His character in what we know as the Ten Commandments (Exodus 20:1-17). This sin leads to spiritual death and separates people from God both in eternity and in their daily lives.

God chose one man, Abraham, and his family to be the source of a blessing that would extend forgiveness and reconciliation to the people He had created (Genesis 15:1-6).

God provided a way to be right before Him through the sacrifice of an unblemished animal. This sacrifice was effective in covering over and removing sin, but it had to be repeated every year (Leviticus 16:15-22).

After nearly two thousand years of atoning for sin through the system of animal sacrifice, God sent His Son, Jesus, fully God and fully man, into the world to live as a human being (Luke 1-2). While Jesus walked the earth, He was without sin (2 Corinthians 5:21). This enabled Him to become the pure sacrifice that would ultimately settle God's wrath against sin.

Jesus was crucified by His own people but rose from the dead after three days (Matthew 27-28; Mark 15-16; Luke 23-24; and John 19-20). This death and resurrection is what allowed Jesus to become the substitute sacrifice for the sins of all people.

This free gift is available to all who wish to receive the grace of God offered in Christ Jesus.

> *For all have sinned and fall short of the glory of God, and all are justified freely by his grace through the redemption that came by Christ Jesus.*
>
> *Romans 3:23-24*

But God demonstrates His own love for us in this: While we were still sinners, Christ died for us.

Romans 5:8

For the wages of sin is death, but the gift of God is eternal life in Christ Jesus our Lord.

Romans 6:23

If you declare with your mouth, "Jesus is Lord," and believe in your heart that God raised Him from the dead, you will be saved. For it is with your heart that you believe and are justified, and it is with your mouth that you profess your faith and are saved.

Romans 10:9-10

For it is by grace you are saved, through faith—and this is not of yourselves, it is the gift of God—not by works, so that no one can boast.

Ephesians 2:8-9

At one time we too were foolish, disobedient, deceived and enslaved by all kinds of passions and pleasures. We lived in malice and envy, being hated and hating one another. But when the kindness and love of God our Savior appeared, He saved us, not because of righteous things we had done, but because of His mercy. He saved us through the washing of rebirth and renewal by the Holy Spirit, whom He poured out on us generously through Jesus Christ our Savior.

Titus 3:3-6

Receiving Christ as your Savior is the first step. It is the only way to peace with God. Jesus says, "I am the Way, the Truth, and the Life. No one comes to the Father except through me" (John 14:6). Salvation is received through faith in the work of Jesus on the cross. The process is as simple as A, B, C:

> **A – Acknowledge:** Admit you are a sinner who is separated from God and need the salvation brought by His Son, Jesus Christ.

> **B – Believe:** Trust that the death and resurrection of Jesus satisfied God's wrath against sin once and for all.

> **C – Confess:** State your helpless case before God and ask Him for forgiveness and help to live a life that is pleasing to Him.

Inviting Jesus to live in you is as simple as praying a prayer like the one below.

> *God, I acknowledge that I am a person who has sinned against You. My sins have separated me from You, and I need the salvation of Jesus to restore me. I believe the death and resurrection of Jesus satisfied your wrath against sin. I believe Jesus' sacrificial death covers over and removes my sin as well. I confess that I have done nothing to deserve Your mercy and forgiveness, but I call upon You to act on Your great love and forgive me. Help me to turn from selfish living and seek to please You in the choices I make.*

Selected Bibliography

Barker, Kenneth, Donald Burdick, John Stek, Walter Wessel, and Ronald Youngblood, eds. *The NIV Study Bible*. Grand Rapids, MI: Zondervan, 1995.

Booker, Richard. *Celebrating Jesus in the Biblical Feasts*. Shippensburg, PA: Destiny Image Publishers, 2008.

LaSor, William Sanford, David Allan Hubbard, and Frederic William Bush. *Old Testament Survey: The Message, Form, and Background of the Old Testament*. Grand Rapids, MI: William B. Eerdmans Publishing Company, 1996.

Lucado, Max. *Traveling Light*. Nashville, TN: Thomas Nelson, 2001.

MacArthur, John. *The MacArthur Bible Commentary*, Nashville, TN: Thomas Nelson, 2005.

MacArthur, John. *The MacArthur New Testament Commentary: Matthew*. Chicago: Moody Press, 1985.

Robinson, Barbara. *The Best Christmas Pageant Ever*. New York: Harper Row Publishers, 1971.

Strobel, Lee. *The Case for Christmas*. Grand Rapids, MI: Zondervan, 1998.

Wright, Christopher J. H. *Knowing Jesus through the Old Testament*. Downers Grove, IL: IVP Academic, 1992.

The author is indebted to scores of other pastors and authors whose accurate teaching of the Word of God has impacted her study. Among them are Dr. Harry Shields, Dr. Danny Leavins, Dr. Mark Harris, and Rick Iglesias.

Songs

Angels from the Realms of Glory – Henry T. Smart, Public Domain.

Be Still My Soul – Katharina Von Schlegel; translated by Jane L. Borthwick, Public Domain.

Come Thou Long Expected Jesus – Charles Wesley, Public Domain.

Deck the Halls – Welsh Carol, Public Domain.

For Unto Us a Child is Born – Charles Jennens and George F. Handel, Public Domain.

Go Tell It on the Mountain – John W. Work Jr., Public Domain.

God Rest Ye Merry Gentlemen – author unknown, Public Domain.

Good Christian Men Rejoice – Latin Carol, translated by John M. Neale, Public Domain.

Hallelujah Chorus – Charles Jennens and George F. Handel, Public Domain.

Hark! The Herald Angels Sing – Charles Wesley, Public Domain.

How Firm a Foundation – C. Michael Hawn, Public Domain.

How Great Our Joy! – German Carol, Public Domain.

It is Well with My Soul – Horatio G. Spafford, Public Domain.

Jesus What a Friend for Sinners – J. Wilbur Chapman, Public Domain.

Joy to the World – Isaac Watts, Public Domain.

Lo How a Rose E'er Blooming – German Hymn, Public Domain.
'

Over the River and Through the Woods – Lydia Maria Child, Public Domain.

O Come All Ye Faithful – C. Frederick Oakeley and John Francis Wade, Public Domain.

O Come, O Come Emmanuel – Latin Hymn, Public Domain.

O for a Thousand Tongues to Sing – Charles Wesley, Public Domain.

O Holy Night – John S. Dwight, Public Domain.

O Little Town of Bethlehem – Louis Henry Redner and Phillips Brooks, Public Domain.

Silent Night – Franz Gruber, Public Domain.

Sing We Now of Christmas – French Carol, Public Domain.

The Solid Rock – William B. Bradbury and Edward Mote, Public Domain.

'Tis So Sweet to Trust in Jesus – Louisa M.R. Snead and William J. Kirkpatrick, Public Domain.

Trust and Obey – John H. Sammis and Daniel B. Towner, Public Domain.

We Three Kings – John Henry Hopkins Jr., Public Domain.

What Can I Give Him? – Christina Rossetti, Public Domain.

What Child is This? – William Chatterton Dix, Public Domain.

Made in the USA
Middletown, DE
14 November 2018